RED SUN

The Invasion
of Hawai'i
After Pearl Harbor

Richard Ziegler and Patrick M. Patterson

THE
BESS
PRESS

3565 Harding Ave. Honolulu, Hawai'i 96816
808/ 734-7159   www.besspress.com

Design and layout: Carol Colbath

Ziegler, Richard.
    Red sun : the invasion of Hawai'i after
Pearl Harbor / Richard Ziegler and Patrick M.
Patterson.
        p. cm.
    Includes bibliography.
    ISBN 1-57306-133-6
    1. Pearl Harbor (Hawaii), Attack on, 1941 -
Fiction. 2. World War, 1939-1945 - Campaigns -
Pacific Area - Fiction. 3. Hawaii - Fiction.
I. Patterson, Patrick M. II. Title
PS3576.I33.R43 2001   813.54-dc20

A note on Hawaiian diacriticals: Although the 'okina and kahakō were not in wide
use during the time period covered by this book, they are included here to clarify
meaning.

Printed in the United States of America

To our fathers' generation, on both sides of the conflict,
who lived through or died in the Great Pacific War

Acknowledgments

We especially recognize Hector Bywater, who first foresaw the coming Great Pacific War, accurately predicted its stages and outcome, and influenced both Japanese and American naval planning. We would like to thank our families, especially Takako, Matthew, and Tomoko, Ann Ziegler, and our friends and colleagues for their support in the writing of this work. Special thanks are in order to Cynthia Smith and Kalani Fujiwara for their review and suggestions. Of course we take full responsibility for any errors, opinions, characters, and descriptions in the book.

CONTENTS

Introduction

A few words are in order about what we have written in this work, and why. Until recently, the genre of "alternative history"—what might have happened—has been shunned by serious historians and largely left to science fiction writers. Recently, however, the genre has been popularized, and legitimized, by reputable, even renowned, historians. *What If?*, edited by Robert Cowley, features chapters by Stephen Ambrose, John Keegan, David McCullough, and James McPherson, among others, on the alternative outcomes of great battles in world history. Other works in this genre currently on bookshelves are *Virtual History*, by Niall Ferguson, *The Hinge Factor: How Accident, Chance, and Stupidity Have Changed History*, by Erik Durschmeid, and *Almost History*, compiled by Roger Bruns. This genre has interested us also, and we have incorporated the theme of alternative outcomes into our book as well, believing that the intentional creation of irony, through the description of events that occur quite differently from what the reader expects, deserves a prominent place in the study of history.

We have taken this approach one step further by writing fiction. We think of it not as historical fiction, but rather "fictional history." What we have written, we believe, is not just plausible, but probable. The events, policies, and actions of the imagined Japanese capture and occupation of Hawai'i are based on what the Japanese military forces actually did elsewhere in Asia and the Pacific during the Great Pacific War. For example, the restoration of the Hawaiian monarchy fits the pattern of the puppet emperor Pu Yi in the Japanese colony of Manchukuo (Manchuria). The break-up of the Big Five is based on Japanese war plans for Hawai'i, had they won the Battle of Midway. Our descriptions of Japanese defenses and battles with the United States are based on defenses and battles elsewhere in the Pacific and what were chillingly real possibilities for Hawai'i early in the war.

In our account of what might have happened, familiar landmarks are placed in new contexts: Koko Crater becomes Mount Suribachi, and Diamond Head, that symbol of a paradise of the Pacific to tourists all over the world, takes on a new and tragic dimension. To imagine what an all-out battle for O'ahu would have been like in World War II, one has only to look at Okinawa. To imagine what would have happened to Honolulu, one has only to look at Manila in 1945. Sources and resources can be found in the bibliography. We hope these will be especially useful to teachers who might use this book to stimulate an interest in history in their students. Field trips to the imagined battle sites and scenes of action, and role-playing might also have this effect.

The story is told through three alternating, interlocking viewpoints. We call these viewpoints Vignettes, Vistas, and Voices. All are short, dramatic chapters with powerful images and events in which the roles of players on different sides are sometimes reversed. The Vignettes are narrow, focused narratives—events seen through a "zoom lens," if you will. The Vista chapters provide the big picture, in sweeping narratives of time and space, conflict and change, as presented by a fictional historian. Finally, the Voices are a single participant's view of things. Three generations of a single AJA (Americans of

Japanese Ancestry) family illustrate how individuals actually "experience" history, how people are swept up and along by big historical events, as in the swift current of a mighty river.

Although the focus is on World War II, the events span a century, from 1868 to 1968, intertwining the histories of Japan and Hawai'i, and the historian whose lectures make up the Vistas chapters is describing events from a present-day perspective. We have included many subtle historical references that "historical detectives" may enjoy uncovering. (Many of these references are explained in the Notes at the end of the book.)

December 7, 2001, is the sixtieth anniversary of the attack on Pearl Harbor. The Great Pacific War ended fifty-six years ago, and the veterans of the war are passing away at the rate of one thousand a day! In a few years, there will be no one left who remembers these tragic, horrific, and heroic events. We hope this small work will serve as a "window into the past," and help keep alive historical memory. Our goal is not to inflame public opinion, but rather to preserve a record of what was— and might have been.

In chapter 8, the historian mentions the "hinge of history." A "hinge event" is a historical event out of the ordinary—one that alters the trajectory of time, of a country's basic direction. The American Civil War is the major hinge event in American history; on this most historians would agree. Pearl Harbor and World War II were hinge events in the transformation of Hawai'i from a feudal, plantation colony to a pluralistic, democratic state. In Hawai'i's history in the twentieth century, the hinge event that might have been, that would have even more profoundly altered the islands' social, economic, and political system had it happened (and it almost did), was the Japanese invasion and occupation in World War II, and the inevitable American counterattack. This is what we have taken up as the subject of our "fictional history." And the hinge is the hinge of a butterfly's wing.

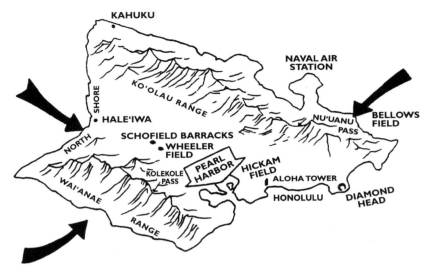

THE JAPANESE INVASION, 1942

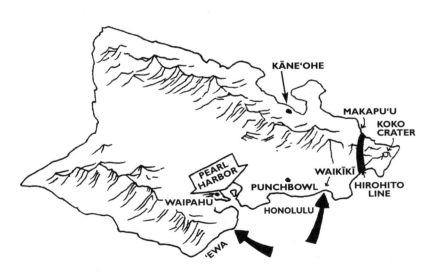

THE AMERICAN INVASION, 1945

VIGNETTES

1
Day of Infamy

November 1941

In the canopy of a steamy Brazilian jungle, sixty feet in the sky, a monarch butterfly flapped its wings. The few molecules of air it disturbed bounced off others, in a random way. The butterfly didn't even lift off the leaf upon which it had alighted. But perhaps the small eddy of air caused the movement of larger flows, until a wind reached the Central Pacific Ocean, where it collided with another wind—one that was in the process of forming a spiral over an unusually cold area of ocean. Because of this meeting of winds, a tropical storm failed to form in the Pacific in early December. Because of this small movement, the USS *Enterprise* was not delayed in its return to O'ahu on December 7, and arrived, nearly perfectly on schedule, at 0600 hours.

December 7, 1941.
Akagi, 200 miles northeast of O'ahu

Planes lined the deck, their props fanning a good breeze aft as *Akagi* swung into the wind for take-off. In the distance, although they could not be seen, *Hiryu, Soryo, Kaga, Zuikaku,* and *Shokaku* were all performing the same maneuver, decks loaded with aircraft ready to leap into the sky. As the bow came 'round, the order to launch was given to the first in line on each vessel, and engines roared as they pulled their charges into the still dark sky in the first seconds of a historic flight.

The pilot of the second Kate off the *Akagi,* Lieutenant Nakajima, didn't even spare a glance for the carrier as he lifted off and headed for the rendezvous point, where nearly a dozen planes of various types were already circling and beginning to form up. He was all focus and excitement. This was what they had practiced for: the torpedo pilots, working for months to modify the designs of their fish and their approach techniques so they could successfully hit targets in the shallow thirty-five-foot water of Pearl Harbor—something every naval aviator in the world believed couldn't be done; the dive-bomber crews, Nakajima's included, memorizing ships, positions, directions, and practicing technique until their bodies were numb. All for this. This was the chance, he knew, to secure the empire of Japan and to strike a blow for the glory of the homeland and the emperor. He was ready, even if he didn't come back, to face down the Americans in their own backyard and force them to see the error of their attempts to isolate Japan.

As the last of the 182 planes of the first wave, including Zero fighters, torpedo bombers, and Kates, formed up on Fuchida, the flight leader, Nakajima wore a grin ear to ear—not of menace, but of anticipation. They were off. He heard his radio operator request permission to take up their post as wing-leader. He gulped air through a dust-dry throat as his plane passed that of Fuchida. He could even see the legendary flyer and strategist in the back seat of his Kate—or rather, could see his silhouette—as they flew by to take station—and honor—in preparation for the raid.

They flew in low over the Ko'olau Mountains, then over a broad plain and over another set of knife-sharp peaks Nakajima knew were called the 'Ewa Range, then began their swing in toward Pearl Harbor. No American planes rose up to greet them, and as the death-trap bay came into clear view, he again gulped as he heard Fuchida radio back to the *Akagi* the phrase denoting achievement of complete surprise: *tora, tora, tora.* The fight was about to begin.

December 7, 1941, 0600 hours. CV-6, USS *Enterprise*

At 0600, Vice Admiral William Halsey was standing on the flying bridge of his flagship, the USS *Enterprise*. Halsey had been awake for two hours already when the flattop finally reached its mooring station, west of Ford Island in Pearl Harbor, very near the old battleship *Utah*. By 0630, he was downing his last cup of Cook's Assistant Brady's coffee, and standing in the rear of a motor launch on the way to his office to begin composing his report. *Enterprise* was in the process of shutting down her boilers, her crew already clamoring for shore passes. At 0755, Halsey was deep in thought when he heard the thunder. Looking out his window, he saw the red sun that was used by the Japanese navy on planes barreling by overhead. He let out a not-so-uncommon "damn." Then, forgetting his cap, he rushed out of the office to find a launch.

Onboard *Enterprise*, as on so many of the other ships anchored in Pearl Harbor, reaction was surprisingly swift, even if preparations and manpower were inadequate. Gunners on the *Aylwin*, almost next door, and on the *Nevada* had opened fire at the Japanese aircraft less than five minutes after the attack had begun. That was too late to save *Oklahoma* or *California*, of course. The antiaircraft fire was clearly disorganized, and insufficient. At this point, no U.S. aircraft could be seen among the wings overhead. Nevertheless, soon two Japanese planes had been brought down. The cruiser *St. Louis*, one of the newest and most capable ships in Pearl, and the destroyer *Aylwin*, nearby, were getting underway and heading toward the harbor entrance—a narrow, shallow slit between two arid peninsulas on the south coast of Oʻahu.

Enterprise, which had arrived only two hours ago and was still in operation, boilers not yet shut down, was one of the first of the big ships to get underway. Before Halsey could find his launch, the commander of the *Enterprise*, Captain George D. Murray, had recognized that *Enterprise* needed to get to the open ocean, where full speed, maneuvering room, and the advantage of increased distance would help her avoid bombs and torpedoes. He also noted that the Japanese, incredibly, were getting torpedo hits in less than forty feet of water.

With nearly a full crew on board, *Enterprise* was one of the readiest ships in the harbor and probably the most organized of all the ships visible. As her guns blazed away, her giant screws began to push the behemoth out toward the narrow mouth of Pearl.

It was clear she was a target. A torpedo meant for her splashed and turtled *Utah* within the first few minutes of the attack. *Enterprise*, moving forward, turned 180 degrees and made for the southern channel around Ford Island. Captain Murray had reasoned, rightly as it turned out, that going the opposite way would bring her through another gauntlet of heavy fire as she passed Battleship Row. Taking her around the southern channel would at least force the Japanese planes to divert from their route to get at the carrier. The more obstacles he could put in their way, the better.

On the opposite side, *Nevada* had got up steam as well. Through some of the haze, Captain Murray could see the battleship try to negotiate its own way to the open sea. Guns blazing, a moving *Nevada* had become a concentrated target—as if the bees had found the hand stealing their honey. Dive-bombing Kates and torpedo-bombers swarmed over the *Nevada*, causing serious damage, seen and unseen. Finally, worried that his vessel might be sunk in the exit channel, the commander of *Nevada* beached his vessel before even trying the difficult negotiation. This act drew a sigh of relief from the captain of *Enterprise*. The channel was clear for his attempt. He had a full head of steam, plenty of bunker, and no damage yet, despite the best efforts of the Japanese naval aviators. And he had to give them credit. They obviously knew what they were doing.

December 7, 1941, 0845 hours. Japanese dive-bomber

Lieutenant Nagashima saw the flattop move around toward the southern channel and the entrance to Pearl Harbor. Early morning reconnaissance had found the *Enterprise* in the harbor. This was an unexpected prize, since information even as late as last night had said there were no carriers in Pearl. He fingered the postcard of Waikīkī on his instrument panel, kept there for luck. This was the opportunity to achieve a major victory here. To sink an aircraft carrier would be a major blow to the U.S. Pacific Fleet and send a clear message about the power of the Japanese navy. He steered his plane toward the deck of the ship. The journey took only a few seconds at twelve thousand feet, and he had to keep his eye on the prize as he began his descent. By the time the bombardier released the weapon on the belly of the plane, the carrier had come considerably closer to the mouth of the harbor. Nakajima dived into the flak, deep within the range of the carrier's guns, and the weapon was released and completed its final flight while the pilot was still pulling out of the dive and beginning to think of avoiding shells. His bombardier and radioman were the two who noticed a bloom of dust, then red flames, then smoke amidships on *Enterprise*'s flight deck.

Others in Nakajima's flight followed, and soon the water around *Enterprise*, as she tried desperately to reach open sea, was full of white impact rings, and explosions were visible on her deck more and more frequently. The great ship was hit astern of the flight deck, in the midst of a starboard turn into the entrance channel to Pearl Harbor, and was apparently unable to pull out of it. Her move to starboard slowed, presenting the perfect opportunity for three other Kates, who lined up their hits squarely along the deck—one more astern, one more amidships, and one near the part of the flight deck that overhung the bow. These had a devastating effect, but the view was soon lost to the pilots in a cloud of black smoke and turbulent, superheated air.

December 7, 1941, 0847 hours.
Pearl Harbor dock

Vice Admiral William Halsey stood on the dock with a curse stuck in his throat. His ship was the most battle-ready, he knew. His Battle Order Number 1, though it had drawn some shocked responses from his crew, had set the *Enterprise* on a wartime footing on its outward voyage to ferry a marine fighter squadron to Wake Island at the end of November. The crew was expecting a fight, and was probably still on pins and needles from the drills he had sent them through. He knew *Enterprise* was ready to fight. He also knew she was a sitting duck in the middle of Pearl during an air attack.

Halsey looked up as a plane bearing the red circles of the empire of Japan on its wings screamed over the dry docks on the east end of the harbor and loosed a torpedo in the direction of one of the battleships. He almost laughed in disbelief, but a cold knot formed in his stomach as a plume of smoke, white water, and debris showed him—and he only needed to be shown once—that the Japanese could use torpedoes at this depth. He was dumbfounded, and even angrier that there were no launches to take him out to his ship. He would have swum out if he thought he could make it. Probably be picked up by one of the launches out on rescue duty if he tried. He turned with a grim smile, knowing the competence of *Enterprise*'s crew. Halsey decided to look for a different place where he might be useful, and prayed that the *Enterprise* would make it out to safety, so she could come back and pick him up, dammit, and they could start getting even. It was the last thought he had.

As he turned to go back up the dock, dive-bombers centered the two fuel tank farms on the east end of Pearl Harbor in their sites, and let go a barrage of incredibly accurate bombs. The tank farms, five hundred million gallons of marine bunker and aviation fuel, went up with the power of a minor earthquake, and the shaking caused relatively large waves in the normally calm harbor. As flames erupted from shattered tanks, the concussion shook Halsey's dock violently. Halsey was thrown off the dock and into the shallow water. He broke his leg in the fall, but he never registered the pain as his head came into violent contact with the dock. Halsey lived for a few more seconds, but never regained consciousness before a major artery in his brain exploded from the sudden impact, killing him. With that, the acknowledged master of naval tactics in the Pacific Theater was taken out of the fight before the fight really even began, another of the nearly five thousand in Hawai'i who didn't live to see the end of this "Day of Infamy."

December 7, 1941, 0857 hours. USS *Enterprise*

The effect of the dive-bombers was devastating. Bombs that penetrated the heavily armored deck of battleships like *Arizona* made it through *Enterprise*'s flight deck and slid deep within her to smash drive shafts. The bomb that hit farthest astern obliterated the controlling mechanism for one of the huge rudders and, forcing the propeller and shaft into it, jammed it in the port position, turning the ship to starboard. Thus the ship, directly across the channel of the harbor's mouth, turned and slowed, aligned perfectly with the line of attack of the Japanese Kates.

The amidships bombs did the most damage, with a pressure wave causing plates beneath the waterline to bulge outward, then buckle inward, releasing a rush of water pressure. The stern bomb slammed into the engine room and opened up the furnaces to the world. Scores of men were immolated before the fuel caught fire, and free cams and pistons as big as small automobiles began to smash through the other machinery and bulkheads nearby.

The foreship bomb hit the magazine. Most of the weaponry stored there was "safed" ordnance for aircraft, and since *Enterprise* did not carry the huge twelve- and fourteen-inch guns of the battleships, there were few bags of explosive black powder. So the explosions were smaller and less spectacular than those destroying *California*, *Oklahoma*, and *Arizona* on Battleship Row. They were enough, however, to open the bulkheads and the hull from near the waterline up to the main deck. *Enterprise* began to settle into the mud, thirty-five feet below the surface, bow first.

With such a low depth, some continuing forward momentum, and the suction power of the muck at the bottom of Pearl, it was not long before *Enterprise* had become an effective roadblock, trapping all other vessels inside the confines of the harbor and creating a turkey shoot for the Japanese. Worse, perhaps, those vessels that did make it out no longer had a home. Most were low on bunker, having not had time or orders to take on any new prior to the attack, and low on stores, including fresh water and food. They would have to return to Hawai'i, with little or no fleet or aircraft to defend them as they sat waiting for a new place to fuel and provision, and for a new mission. They would be sitting ducks if another attack occurred after their return.

The superstructure of *Enterprise* was visible from nearly any point near the beach in Honolulu. Tilted awkwardly, with rigging hanging helter-skelter, and huge misshapen pieces missing from its railings, windows broken, it reminded the salvage crews, as they began to try to right *Oklahoma* and refloat *Nevada*, that all their work would mean little if *Enterprise* could not be moved. Salvage and return to the fleet was out of the question. Surveys after the all-clear had been sounded confirmed that *Enterprise* was a total loss.

December 7, 1941, 0900 hours. North Pacific Ocean

Hachiman, god of war, was surely smiling on the Japanese that December morning. As the third wave of Japanese attack aircraft returned to their carriers, they spotted the USS *Lexington* on her return leg from Midway. By midmorning, *Lexington* was burning, limping back toward the West Coast of the American mainland so badly damaged that she could not even recover the few aircraft she'd gotten up to defend herself. Her pilots had to ditch their planes in the sea and await rescue boats from the crippled carrier.

American forces in the Pacific had, in the space of three hours, been devastated by the victorious Japanese.

VIGNETTES

2
Raising the Sun

April 29, 1942

The dilapidated, begrimed renaissance facade of the 'Iolani Palace stood straight, tall, silent that Saturday afternoon. The sun shone brilliantly, golden in the last half of its arc toward the western horizon—toward Japan.

One thousand soldiers lined the walk to the main entry of the former palace of the kings and queens of old Hawai'i. One thousand soldiers in khaki, rifles on shoulders, uniforms as crisp as the situation allowed, stared straight forward, standing at parade rest in eerie silence as the Stars and Stripes was lowered from the flagpole. The only sound, heard by those closest to the flag crew, was the clinking of hooks against each other, and a shraaap shraaap that sounded like the closing of drapes on a silent Sunday afternoon.

When the flag was down, it was folded in the traditional triangle. Silently, the officer in command of the color guard, Lieutenant Kimura, turned sharply on his heels, took two steps, and placed the flag in the hands of the lieutenant governor of the Territory of Hawai'i. He bowed, then turned again, sharply. Facing the one thousand, he said, in a loud, controlled voice,

"*Kiyotsuke!* Attention!" He then turned toward a man in a khaki uniform with braid on its shoulders, as the one thousand came to attention as one. Kimura bowed again. The general nodded his head. Kimura, in a swift, practiced motion, reached across his abdomen with his right hand, quickly drew his officer's sword, and held it upright in front of his right shoulder. Facing the flag crew, he swung the sword groundward in a sudden stroke. The band just in front of the flagpole began to play "Kimigayo," the anthem of the empire of Japan, as the *hinomaru* (rising sun) flag, with a single red circle on a white field, rose to the top of the pole.

The one thousand stood unmoving. Their officers' hands went up in crisp salutes. A tall, dark-haired young man standing to the left of the general stood at attention, in a dark formal suit. He appeared to be ill at ease.

As the anthem ended, the general stepped to a microphone at the podium on the balcony of 'Iolani Palace. He bowed slightly to the one thousand, and turned to give a deep, respectful bow to the tall young man in the dark suit.

"Your majesty," he said, "*Hon jitsu, hawai ōkoku ha, jiū ni narimas*! Today, Hawai'i becomes free! Welcome, to the Greater East Asia Co-Prosperity Sphere! Through the grace and wisdom of our emperor in Tokyo, the Japanese army has been sent, and has successfully helped the kingdom of Hawai'i to liberate itself from the oppression of the United States. We have come, according to the request made to our great Meiji emperor sixty years ago by Hawai'i's great King Kalākaua, to bring Hawai'i into its rightful place within Asia. Asia for the Asians!"

A cheer went up from the one thousand, but they quickly quieted down as the general motioned he had more to say.

"With the signing of this document"—he held up a large white sheet covered with Japanese writing—"the United States of America will formally cede all control over the Hawaiian Islands to Japan. This document is one of unconditional surrender for the United States."

Another cheer went up, this time lasting slightly longer as some of the one thousand lifted rifles into the air.

"Will the representative of the government of the United States of America please step forward." He said it in Japanese, but an aide who stood near a short, but burly white man whispered a translation into the white man's ear.

John McMillan Anderson, lieutenant governor of the Territory of Hawai'i, and highest ranking survivor among representatives of the U.S. government, stepped forward. He was given a fountain pen, and he stepped again toward a low table on the balcony. There he placed his signature, in a shaking hand, on two documents, identical in that one was in English, the other in Japanese. After finishing his signature, he stepped back, nervous, and then, remembering the pen, stepped forward again to replace it on the table. He placed it very deliberately, hardly believing he could still stand, exactly between the two documents, then stepped back. As he did so, his elbows were taken by two Japanese guards, and they immediately marched him off the dais and away from the ceremony.

The general, Mori was his family name, stepped forward and, taking a *fude* brush, dipped it in ink and brushed his name, in strong even strokes, in Chinese characters, on both documents. As he set the brush down and stood, the silence virtually crackled with energy. The one thousand were as unmoving as stones, the wind passing them as it did the edifice in front of which they stood, with no effect.

Kimura stepped forward, sheathed his sword in a swift, practiced motion, placed both of his hands at his side, and in a tremendous shout said, *"Tenno Heika, banzai!"*

The one thousand, throwing both hands high in the air, repeated *"Banzai, banzai, banzai!"*

General Mori, tears in his eyes, but standing tall, nodded to Kimura, who faced the flag crew again and unsheathed his sword. Mori said, "Your Majesty, Japan has no interest in making

Hawai'i a part of her empire. Hawai'i and Japan have always had a mutually supportive relationship. Our great Emperor Meiji was unable, due to diplomatic considerations in 1894, to accept a marriage of Hawaiian and Japanese royal lines. Nevertheless, he did consider himself a brother to the king of Hawai'i. Now that the diplomatic situation has changed, our emperor desires to see his brother, the king of Hawai'i, return to his rightful position as head of state. Please accept the kingdom of Hawai'i, returned to you, as a gift from the emperor of Japan. As a further show of his reverence for you, and his care for the freedom of the people of Hawai'i, the wise emperor has directed that the power of Japan's military might be at your disposal, to prevent any attempts by your former oppressors to steal again what they stole in 1898. I, my fellow commanders, and our men and weapons are at your disposal, sir."

As Mori said these last words, Kimura once again brandished his sword, and as the band played the anthem of the kingdom of Hawai'i, the Hawaiian flag was raised on a second flagpole to a parallel height with the Japanese flag. This was the same flag that had been drawn down in 1898 by the Color Guard of the United States Army New York Volunteer Infantry upon the kingdom's annexation by the Americans. The young king, Stephen Kamāmalu, who had said not a word, stood at strict attention, facing the flag, and watched it rise. His face was tense, held in a stern gaze, his mind apparently full of the implications of this moment. As the Hawaiian flag, with the Union Jack in its upper left corner, and broad red, white, and blue stripes on its main field, reached the top, he bowed to Mori. Then he took the podium, and said simply, first in the Hawaiian language, then in English, and finally in Japanese, "Thanks are due to the great emperor of Japan, and to the Japanese army and navy. I hereby proclaim the restoration of the kingdom of Hawai'i."

The one thousand, at the simple motion of Kimura raising his sword once more to his shoulder, bent on one knee, heads down. The officers remained standing, but each and every one, including Mori, saluted. Kimura placed his sword before his face in a cavalry salute.

'Iolani Palace, dilapidated, long abused by the Territorial Government of the United States, was engulfed in a deep silence. Trade winds whistled past the still one thousand, ruffling hair, turning reverent eyes to the new view of Honolulu Harbor. There, in the distance, Aloha Tower stood shattered, the clock face gone, the tower itself a hollow column of brick, piercing the late-afternoon sky and rending the clouds with its jagged edges. Just beyond, in clear sight and nearly as tall, stood the flight control tower on the superstructure of the great aircraft carrier *Akagi*, the naval sunburst cloud flapping, whipping in the trades in counterpoint to the ragged tower and the *hino-maru* flag now floating above the flaking, grayed 'Iolani Palace.

This sight drew an almost spiritual sigh from many in the ranks of the one thousand, as they exulted in their victory and grieved for the dead, who'd paid hero's dues on both sides of the fight. The Americans, each privately thought, hungry and tired as they must have been, had shown they were not the soft creatures of material comfort the soldiers had been led to expect. Still, victory was victory, and such errors in information could now be forgiven. They had won. The Japanese Imperial Army and Navy, together, were now in possession of the Hawaiian Islands. Their power, their worthiness, was now before the world, proven with the stark evidence of sacrifice and victory. Yes, many of the one thousand cried privately, keeping the tears inside, but crying tears of joy nonetheless.

Mori, privately, was jubilant. The Japanese Empire in the Pacific was now complete. The Americans had been defeated, and their forward bases all taken. There was simply no way they could replace their losses and make any meaningful moves against Japan now. They would have to see the folly of resistance, and accept the new world order as it was presented to them. Their only choice was to stop their ineffectual threats and trade embargoes and negotiate with the Japanese. Support for China from the U.S. West Coast was nearly impossible, even if the carriers had survived. As it was, only one was known to have been afloat on December 7 when the Japanese fleet left the area of the Hawaiian Islands, and that one, *Lexington*, was on fire and listing badly. Nothing was known about the carrier, but it seemed unlikely it had made the long trip to San Diego Bay. Mori silently said a prayer to the gods for those brave Americans who must have died trying to save their ship, somewhere in the mid-Pacific. He did not grieve, though. There was nothing sad about giving one's life in service to one's nation—even one as corrupt and soft as the United States. Those sailors were heroes, each and every one.

It was the survivors whom Mori despised, those who had fought for their country, and then, when all hope was gone, instead of going out in glory, fighting to the moment of death, had surrendered. They had given up all honor, all right to glory, all right to expect to be treated as warriors as soon as they had ceased to be warriors—on the field of battle, disgracing their uniforms and themselves by giving in to defeat before all was lost. Mori had no sympathy for them, and he did not care what happened to them. They were a nuisance. He could not kill them, but he could keep them out of the way, and he would.

Mori looked at the faces of the one thousand as they treasured the moment, before he dismissed them and began his duties as "advisor" to the new king of the Hawaiian Islands. They had fresh young faces again, not the battle-worn frowns he had seen just twenty-four hours ago. They were the jewels in the emperor's crown. He had seen many of them just the day before, taking pictures of each other for family members in front of the hulks of Pearl Harbor. Some smiled and pointed at the wrecked hull of the USS *Enterprise* behind them, sunk in the entrance to Pearl Harbor on December 7, attempting to escape to deep water and maneuverability. Some stood before the twisted superstructure of the mostly submerged *Arizona*, or the upturned keel of *Oklahoma*, proud sister ships in the once formidable line of battleships in the U.S. Pacific Fleet. These boys had sacrificed so much to be here—friends, limbs, many lives. They would likely sacrifice more, he thought, before this was over. But for today . . .

"Dismissed!" he shouted at Kimura. Kimura turned to the one thousand, tears still in his eyes, and shouted "dismissed!" to them. They turned right as one, to face the palace, the restored king, and their theater commander. They bowed in unison, then turned as a body to face the rear and began marching off to the dispersal area one hundred meters down the road, rank by rank, in perfect step. The day was a success. Hawai'i belonged to the Japanese.

VOICES

3
The Grandfather's Story, Part 1

Let me tell you about Hawai'i and Japan's common destiny through the story of my own life.

I was born sometime in the summer of 1868, in a small, poor village of farmers on the island of Kyushu. That was the first year of Emperor Meiji, and the beginning of great changes in Japan. Before that, Japan was ruled by the Tokugawa Shogunate for more than 250 years. The Tokugawa kept out the *gaijin* barbarians who had conquered China and the rest of Asia by driving out the Christian missionaries, banning guns and things foreign, and closing Japan to the outside world. As a result, Japan fell behind with weapons and machinery, so when the American Perry came to Japan more then ten years before I was born, the shogun and his *daimyō* lords and *samurai* soldiers could not keep him out. The shogun was overthrown by the "outside clans" who supported the new boy emperor in Kyoto. He was brought to Edo to live in the shogun's castle the year I was born, and great changes came to Japan.

When I was growing up, men from my village who had been to the cities told of new factories and railroads, a new constitution and laws, a new system of banks and a new money called the *yen*. The first change we felt in my village was the building of a school. Even before then, my father and older brothers gave me *shushin*—strict moral training, with devotion to my family, my ancestors, and the emperor. Some of my earliest memories are of my father teaching me to honor, love, and sacrifice for my homeland. My older brother was drafted into the new army, and he was killed fighting the old-guard *samurai* under Saigo Takamori, who rebelled against the new way of things. I had no desire to be a soldier after that, and part of the "blood tax," as my father called it.

The boys of my village had very strict schooling for eight years, and I learned to read, write, and do math. One day someone brought a copy of a book called *The New Hawai‘i* to the village. When my turn to read it came, I couldn't put it down. It described a beautiful, pleasant life on the sugar plantations of Hawai‘i, across the great eastern sea.

Life in my village was getting harder, despite the new changes under Emperor Meiji, so when I was fifteen I went off on my own to the city of Yokohama. My father could not pay his taxes, and he had to sell off some of his land. I thought I could get a factory job and send him money to buy back his land. The conditions in the textile mill where I worked were very bad, and my place to live was in a crowded set of rooms with many other boys like me. I hated it even worse than working in the rice fields.

So I was in Yokohama in 1881 when King Kalākaua of Hawai‘i came to Japan on his trip around the world. I remember he arrived on a ship called the *Oceanic* in March. Many foreign ships were there to welcome him. They flew Hawaiian flags and gave him a twenty-one–gun salute! There were also hundreds of sampans in the harbor, and the emperor's ship *Mikado* came to invite the king to be a royal guest of the emperor at his summer palace. Then he went to Edo to meet Emperor Meiji himself. There was a big parade as the king rode through the streets in a royal carriage. Throngs of people holding

Japanese and Hawaiian flags greeted the king as he boarded the train to Edo. We heard he even shook hands with His Majesty, and they got along so well that the Hawaiian king stayed ten days, enjoying the dinners, teas, balls, and theater.

We learned later that the king had a special reason for coming to Japan. He was seeking to persuade the government to allow Japanese to go work in Hawai'i. He wanted thousands of workers to come for the new plantations in sugar and pineapples. The king felt a special tie with our emperor. He too was being pressured and threatened by the *gaijin* countries, in trade and other economic matters, to sign "unequal" treaties. We heard that he even proposed a marriage between his young niece Kai'ulani and Crown Prince Komatsu, but nothing ever came of it. The emperor must have agreed to the other things though, because soon recruiting agents came to Japan to sign up workers for Hawaiian plantations. The one I heard described Hawai'i as a paradise, a land of gentle people, where it was always summer. Soon there was a "Hawai'i *netsu*"—an emigration fever—sweeping through the area south of Honshu and Kyushu, around Hiroshima.

I didn't see any future for myself in Japan, so I made up my mind to go to Hawai'i and work for a few years, then return to Japan and help my father as I had planned. I was young then— seventeen—and I was ready for bold action, willing to take a chance. The recruiter said I could save four hundred yen in just three years! A factory worker in Yokohama would have to work maybe ten years to save that much. Many young men like me wanted to go to Hawai'i then; there were almost thirty thousand men applying for the six hundred places in that first batch of workers. I was one of the lucky ones, I thought. I was picked. I didn't even know what a "contract" was, but I signed a three-year contract to earn nine dollars a month!

We had heard stories of an earlier group of Japanese workers who went to Hawai'i on the ship *Scioto* the year I was born. A storm at sea was a bad omen of what was to come. They were treated badly we heard, and most came home disappointed.

We didn't think about that then. We were young and brave, and we had our whole lives in front of us.

VISTAS

4
Ring of Steel

"I have this day assumed the position of military governor of Hawai'i, and have taken charge of the government of the Territory."

- General Walter C. Short, Dec. 7, 1941

Mahalo for this opportunity to present my findings here at the Royal University of Hawai'i, in this lecture series I have titled "The Hinge of Modern Hawai'i." This first lecture is "Ring of Steel."

Short's proclamation to the people of Hawai'i, which I have just quoted, went on to warn that violations of the martial law ordinances would be met by severe punishment and imprisonment by military tribunals. Thus Hawai'i became the first American territory to fall under military rule. The bombs had hardly stopped falling before Governor Poindexter signed a statement that turned over most of the functions of the civilian government to the army. Years later, the Supreme Court declared the imposition of martial law in Hawai'i to be unconstitutional, but on December 7, 1941, there were few dissenters. The fear, panic, and hysteria from the Japanese attack built over the following months as it became clear that the bombing was only the first step in the invasion and conquest of Hawai'i and the Pacific by the Japanese Empire.

The bombs and antiaircraft fire were not confined to the military bases. At least forty antiaircraft shells fell back into the city of Honolulu. In the panic of the attack and rush of the response, many had incorrectly set fuses; one even cratered into the Washington Place grounds, next to the governor's mansion itself! Fires broke out all over town. The largest drove thirty-one families out of thirteen buildings at the intersection of King and McCully streets. Makeshift ambulances rushed through the streets carrying the three hundred injured civilians to hospitals. The two hours of the Japanese attack produced a chaos of falling bombs, flying shrapnel, burning fuel, and wailing sirens, followed by three years of terror, hardship, and profound changes in the historical trajectory of Hawai'i.

Under martial law, civilian courts ceased operation, as military judges and military tribunals took over. The radio stations were shut down for a time, and newspapers came under tight censorship. A six-thirty p.m. curfew was imposed on top of the strict blackout. All labor relations came under the control of the military—jobs and wages were frozen, and absenteeism led to fines or even jail sentences. Prices, food production, public health, even prostitution fell under the authority of the military governor, and a host of new agencies and regulations were created. As onerous as these restrictions and violations of civil liberties were over the next few months, they would pale in comparison to the military rule imposed by the Japanese military officials when Hawai'i became part of the Greater East Asia Co-Prosperity Sphere.

After the initial shock wore off, the dead were buried—the 60 civilians; the 2,400 soldiers, sailors, and marines from Pearl Harbor, Hickam, Schofield, Wheeler, and Kāne'ohe, and from the 18 warships and 200 planes lost; and the 2,109 men from the stricken carrier *Enterprise*, shattered at Pearl. After the graves were filled in, the shovels of O'ahu were put to good use for digging trenches and air raid shelters—in school- and church-yards, behind homes and in front of public buildings. One thousand large public shelters were planned, and about 250 were built before the Japanese bomber forces returned.

The U.S. plans for "Fortress O'ahu" and the "Ring of Steel" around it were crippled and aborted by the devastating attack of December 7 and the follow-up raids that preceded the invasion and occupation of February 1942.

On December 1, 1941, O'ahu represented the greatest concentration of American military power in the world, but of course the United States was ranked only eighteenth in the world, behind even Portugal, at that time! Pearl and the other bases held 10 battleships, 3 carriers with 250 planes, scores of cruisers, dozens of destroyers, and 500 land-based aircraft. Schofield Barracks was America's largest military base, home of the Twenty-fourth and Twenty-fifth Infantry divisions. Their numbers, plus the Hawai'i National Guard, put the island's military manpower at nearly fifty thousand men.

The static coastal defenses protected O'ahu's southern shore, from Honolulu Harbor out to Pearl Harbor. Inside Diamond Head crater, Fort Ruger's eight twelve-inch-caliber mortars could drop 700-pound deck-piercing armor shells almost 14 miles in a near vertical plunging fire. Fort DeRussy's Battery Randolph sported a 2-gun battery of 14-inch guns that could put a 1,500-pound shell through the side of an enemy ship. Fort Armstrong's defenses centered on controlled submarine mines, and Fort Kamehameha at the entrance to Pearl Harbor combined all three offensive capabilities. All four forts were directed in observation, coordination, and targeting by a multileveled bunker structure near the summit of Diamond Head. The big guns of Fort Weaver and Fort Barrette in leeward O'ahu both utilized 16-inch guns that could fire a 2,340-pound shell 28 miles, and a 2,240-pound shell twenty-five miles. In theory, the Fort Weaver guns covered the approach to every beach on O'ahu, with target coordinates from Ka'ena Point stations. Around Oʻahu, 127 fixed coast defense guns and 217 antiaircraft guns were in place, augmented by three thousand artillery pieces and automatic weapons. But all that was not enough.

The overwhelming attack of December 7 changed the balance of power in the eastern Pacific in less than two hours. Eight battleships were out of action, and the carriers were gone—*Enterprise* sunk in the Pearl Harbor channel, *Lexington* aflame and limping back to the West Coast. The dry dock facilities were in ruins, and the oil fuel supplies for the Pacific Fleet and army—4.5 million barrels—were destroyed in the burning tank farm. Worse was to come. Japan possessed the finest fleet of long-distance submarines in the world, and these were now put to use to blockade, isolate, and starve the Hawaiian Islands, as a prelude to invasion. Puny strings of barbed wire along Waikīkī Beach were not going to do the job.

There was a "Ring of Steel" around Oʻahu, but it wasn't the big guns, the rail-mounted artillery pieces, or the mobile troops and their weapons. It was instead the Japanese submarine fleet surrounding Hawaiʻi.

The Hawaiian archipelago extends some fifteen hundred miles in a northwest to southeast direction. Together, the 132 islands, the most isolated set of islands in the world, constitute a landmass of 6,425 miles. Oʻahu, "the Gathering Place," stands at the center of these—the "hub," whose spokes reach out to Asia, America, and Australia. Oʻahu, with only 607 square miles of Hawaiʻi's total land area, is only the third largest of the Hawaiian islands, yet in 1941 was the home of sixty percent of Hawaiʻi's 425,000 people.

Hawaiʻi's geographical isolation, together with her dependency on imported food and fuel, was the weakness in her Ring of Steel. Hawaiʻi-grown food met only a small percentage of local island needs—ten percent of her rice, thirty percent of her fish, forty percent of her meat, and forty percent of her vegetables. The rest came in ships from thousands of miles away—

three million tons annually, in thirty ships every month. This lifeline was now cut by the long range I Class subs of the Combined Fleet. Ten days after the Pearl Harbor attack, a convoy sent from the West Coast to supply and defend Hawai'i was cut off and destroyed. Of the thirty ships sent out, with eight thousand troops and millions of tons of food and oil, only seven escaped the torpedoes. The waters four hundred miles east of Hawai'i were littered with oil slicks and corpses, boxes and barrels. The hope of delivery and rescue in Hawai'i turned to shock and despair as the awful truth of what happened slipped through the web of news censorship military rule had imposed. No other convoy tried to run the gauntlet of *sensuikan* (submarines)!

One success after another created new opportunities for Japan. The sinking of *Enterprise* and near destruction of *Lexington* had emboldened Admiral Nagumo to launch the third wave of attack on December 7. This attack, which torched oil storage tanks and wrecked dry dock facilities, crippled the base. The surviving warships at Pearl were bottled up; the shattered *Enterprise* was the cork, blocking the narrow channel. The ships could neither be repaired nor make an escape without fuel. The oil that in another scenario would have powered battles and victories at Coral Sea and Midway instead rose into the trade winds as greasy black smoke.

Midway, comprising two islets and a surrounding coral reef, lies 1,135 miles northwest of Pearl Harbor—closer to Japan than to the American West Coast. These islets were considered to be the "sentries for Hawai'i," guarding the approaches to O'ahu. In the light of the recent Japanese successes, the islets proved instead to be steppingstones to Hawai'i.

Admiral Isoroku Yamamoto saw the immediate advantage of seizing the lightly defended islands now that the Pacific Fleet was crippled sufficiently to be unable to intervene. The seizure of Midway would further demoralize the American public and leaders. It would, he argued, head off Hawai'i-based aircraft, and Japan's possession of these islands might be the bait to lure the West Coast–based American fleet into a decisive battle. Yamamoto, from the mid-1920s on, envisioned an invasion of Hawai'i itself, with Midway to be used as the staging area. He knew first-hand of America's strength and Japan's weakness in a protracted war of attrition. Only bold military actions followed by skillful diplomacy could lead to a negotiated peace with America favorable to Japan's interest.

Yamamoto was now ready to roll the dice on this essentially defensive gamble. The American garrison on Midway was small enough that it could be taken without the help of the Japanese army, which had great reservations about expansion eastward. Accordingly, he gave orders for the rapid assault on Midway, to keep the momentum of victory going in Japan's favor. The Midway Neutralization Force under Captain Kanamo Konishi, with the destroyers *Ushio* and *Sazanami*, were sent to bombard the air base at Midway and ensure a safe return for Nagumo's fleet. Following Yamamoto's directive, Nagumo sailed for Truk to overhaul the fleet and take on supplies. Japanese regiments from the Caroline and Marshall islands beefed up the invasion force. The replenished fleet sailed eastward once again, for Wake, Johnston, and Midway atolls—the "bridge" for the seizure of Hawai'i. After a brief but furious struggle, Midway was captured on January 7, 1942, one month to the day after the Pearl Harbor attack. With control of the sea and air around Midway, and indeed over Hawai'i, the build-up of men and materiel could proceed.

Midway's immediate advantage was as an "unsinkable aircraft carrier" for the softening up of O'ahu—enabling air assaults on O'ahu's coastal defenses, her guns and forts, her roads and bridges, her bases and barracks. These assaults, combined with the naval blockade, began to rapidly corrode and collapse O'ahu's Ring of Steel. Almost as effective as the physical attrition of O'ahu's concrete and steel defenses was the psychological wearing down of hope and resistance from the daily bombing and shelling from Japanese warships off the coast, now emboldened by the waning defenses. Hope of rescue and relief gave way to resignation and despair. Any chance of reinforcements arriving from twenty-five hundred miles away grew steadily slimmer as Japan tightened her "ring of steel" into an iron noose through January and into February of 1942.

Panic-stricken crowds pushing their way onto the last few miscellaneous ships evacuating to the West Coast resembled the scene in Saigon thirty-one years later. Thousands of mainlanders took their chances with the Japanese submarine blockade to reach the safety of the West Coast, jamming freighters, trawlers, and passenger liners.

The invasion of the Rising Sun, looming over the western horizon, was destined to be the final eastern thrust of an empire that soon stretched from the borders of Siberia to the coast of New Guinea, from central China to the beaches of Waikīkī. In only four months, the Japanese Empire had come to embrace twenty million square miles, an area five times the size of Hitler's empire at its peak.

VOICES

5
The Grandfather's Story, Part 2

We left Japan in early January. I was seventeen years old then, hoping for romance and adventure. Only my younger brother was able to say good-bye to me at the dock. He gave me a small Amida Buddha figure, to watch over me. As the mountains of Japan grew smaller, so did my courage and bravery. Once my homeland was out of sight, I was filled with homesickness. I was soon nostalgic for the rice fields I used to hate so much, and the small village of huts we called home. I could hear the voices of my family, especially my mother, who cried when I had carelessly told her of my plans.

Soon the homesickness was replaced by seasickness as the ocean waves rolled the ship to and fro. Whenever I see a woodblock print of Hokusai's *Great Wave at Kanagawa*, I think of that miserable two-week voyage to Hawai'i on the *City of Tokio*, the steamer that carried the first Japanese workers to Hawai'i. We were the first large contingent—over six hundred men, the rest women and children, nearly one thousand altogether. By the time I left the plantation in 1920, almost two hundred thousand of my fellow Japanese followed our path. But we were the first, the "pioneers," you might say, and we did not know what awaited us.

Many of us had left Japan because our families were poor, and we had dreams of saving money to return to Japan—our home. Some did, but most of us stayed in the new land.

We were really crowded together on that little ship. In the daytime we had to stay below decks in steerage, and only at night were we allowed on deck to breathe fresh cool air. The food was terrible on ship—hard bread, saltfish, some rice and barley. The water was bad, and that made people sick too. The smell of vomit and human waste added to our misery. And there were bedbugs, so we scratched all the time. We Japanese need our daily bath, and that was not possible on the ship. The salt-water cleanings brought relief for only a short while, until the salt burned our bug bites and scratches. We heard later that the first Christian missionaries, who came to Hawai'i from Boston in the United States more than fifty years before us in sailing ships, spent six whole months at sea, going around the terrible Cape Horn. I have to give them credit for that!

Finally, on January 20, 1885, we saw the faint outlines of the green mountains of Hawai'i. We were greeted at the dock by the king, David Kalākaua, because we were the first large group of workers to come. I have to say that at first we were given a special welcome. There was music for us, and *sake*, and we had a Japanese sports festival, and good food. We were served milk, and noodles, and rice cake. We had a sumo match with twenty wrestlers. The planters and government officials even arranged some sightseeing in the city of Honolulu. I especially remember the king's palace and the Royal Hawaiian Hotel. There seemed to be people from all over the world in the streets—Hawaiians, Chinese, and Americans, so different from Japan!

We had landed at the Sand Island quarantine station, where so many of my countrymen were to pass through. The quarantine station was mainly for smallpox. By the time we came to Hawai'i, the Native Hawaiian population was less than one third of what it had been when the first *gaijin*, Captain Cook, sailed to Hawai'i. For Hawaiians, he is what the American Commodore Perry is for us Japanese. Both of them opened the islands to the outside world, but it turned out to be more fortunate for Japan. After the great King Kamehameha died, the weaker sons of the king let the *gaijin*—the haoles as they call them—take over. Earlier, in Japan, the strong Tokugawa Shogunate, started by Ieyasu, kicked the *gaijin* out, especially the Christian missionaries. When the Emperor Meiji came to the throne two hundred years later, we were ready to deal with the Western powers on our own terms, and to learn the secrets of their strength.

After all the festivities, we were marched to the yard near the customhouse, guarded, inspected, then selected for the plantation we had been assigned to. We were divided up by the village or area we were from, and group leaders were appointed or selected. After two weeks crowded together, we had a pretty good idea of who our leaders should be.

I was picked to work at Kahuku plantation. Little did I know that I would spend the next thirty years of my life in that little place, and never return to my village and family. Kahuku is almost fifty miles from Honolulu, on the "windward" side of O'ahu, so we had a long wagon ride up through Nu'uanu Valley and down the Old Pali Road. I was afraid the wagon was going to tumble over the steep cliff! The windward coast was beautiful—sandy beaches, green mountains, fishing coves, and small Hawaiian villages.

When we got to Kahuku, we were exhausted. It was late in the evening, and we single men found ourselves crowded into thatched-roof huts or barracks, six of us in a room barely eight feet by twelve feet! All the Japanese workers were in one camp, while nearby the Hawaiian and Chinese, and later the Filipino workers had their own camp. There were much nicer cottages for the white, skilled workers, and the top managers and supervisors had big white houses up on the hill, with porches or verandas around the outside. The crowded conditions made all of us tense and easily angry. Later, married couples shared small cottages, divided for two families. They were able to build hot bathhouses, or *furo*, and to start gardens and plant trees, raise chickens and ducks.

For us single men, crowded together in the barracks, the cottages seemed like heaven. It was several years before I was to live like that. I was still determined to remain single, to save every dollar I earned and return to Japan a rich man.

VISTAS

6
Eastern Operation

Welcome to the second lecture in the "Hinge of Modern Hawai'i" series. Today's lecture, "The Eastern Operation," deals with Japan's invasion of the Hawaiian Islands. Let me begin with the words of Admiral Yamamoto, spoken at Imperial Japanese General Headquarters, Tokyo.

"Gentlemen, I have called this special meeting this morning to consider a rethinking of our military aims in the Greater East Asian War, in light of a greater, changed balance of forces in the Eastern Pacific Theater. The overwhelming success of Admiral Nagumo's attack on the American forces at Pearl Harbor—twenty-one ships sunk or seriously damaged, including the carriers *Enterprise* and *Lexington*, the entire fuel storage facilities and dry dock facilities for the Pacific Fleet destroyed—and our seizure of Midway, just thirteen hundred miles from O'ahu create the need and opportunity to reformulate our goals and strategies.

"These successes, together with rapid advances against the Anglo-American forces in the Philippines and Southeast Asia, make necessary the shift in men, materiel, and resources from China and Manchuria, where our forces have been bogged down for many years, to the Central and Eastern Pacific Theater. In short we must extend our defensive perimeter to include the Hawaiian Islands!

"On December 9, less than forty-eight hours after the great victory at Pearl Harbor, I instructed my chief of staff to draw up plans for "Eastern Operation"—the invasion of Hawai'i. These islands in Japanese hands would be America's Achilles heel. This advantage will give us several options. First, there is the possibility of luring the remnants of the American Fleet into a decisive battle, as Admiral Togo did with the Russian Fleet at Tsushima in 1905. As you know, this was the prelude to the successful conclusion of that war, granting us control of Korea. The holding of some four hundred thousand American prisoners of war will be the bargaining chip with America for our control of the Western Pacific and Asia. Remember, Hawai'i is just a colony for the United States; a colony is always expendable. If the Americans refuse to reach a satisfactory negotiated settlement, then we have the threat to attack the West Coast, and of course we have cut off their supply line to Australia and denied them a base to launch carrier strikes on our empire.

"I lived in America for many years, and I have seen the vast industrial potential of that continent. Remember, gentlemen, Japan is the size of their one state of California! At all costs, we must avoid a protracted war of attrition against such a power; such a war we would inevitably lose. My studied opinion in our present situation is to initiate bold military action followed up by skillful diplomacy. Our only hope is to make this war too costly for the Americans. We must retain the initiative with aggressive action: keep the United States off balance—*happō yabure*—strike on all sides! The Combined Fleet stands behind me on this approach. I now ask the Imperial Army to join with us in the conquest of Hawai'i. Thank you."

- Notes taken at Admiral Isoroku Yamamoto's briefing before the Imperial Army General Staff, shortly after the attack on Pearl Harbor

The argument and discussion of Yamamoto's ideas apparently went on for several hours, with the usual exhortations to destroy the Anglo-Saxon colonies in Asia and the Pacific. Of course, there were the usual claims that the ultimate victory would be one of the Yamato warrior spirit over American decadence and materialism. In the end, the Army General Staff saw the wisdom of Yamamoto's thinking and, after a long debate, threw its support behind Eastern Operation. The success of the Pearl Harbor attack, and all others throughout Asia and the Pacific in the previous two months, had brought a sense of exhilaration, a relief from the tensions of the previous months, and an end to the strangulation by the Western powers, which were denying Japanese national destiny.

On December 31, 1941, Dairikushi 905—the order for the attack on Hawai'i—went out. For the assault, the Second and the Seventh divisions were to spearhead the diversionary attacks, while the Fifth and Sixth divisions, trained in amphibious warfare, were to launch the main assault. Behind these 88,000 battle hardened troops came 9 carriers, 477 Zeros, 159 bombers, 300 subs, and a host of transport, tanker, and supply ships, all gathered at Midway.

They came at dawn, with the rising sun. Early morning surfers at Mā'ili Beach were taking advantage of a set of big waves from the south when the dots on the western horizon grew larger and larger as a transport ship maneuvered in toward the shoreline. There had been the daily Japanese air attacks on coastal batteries and gun emplacements, only slightly heavier the past week, but the more adventurous surfers had become used to them. The attacks had always been directed at specific targets, and had almost been accepted as part of the Wai'anae coast scene. The surfers had ignored the warnings to stay out of the surf. They threaded their way through the barbed wire strands running the length of the beach, and launched themselves on their longboards into the water.

Now however, as the transport ship drew closer to the shore, it began to disgorge the landing craft full of soldiers, the morning sun glinting off their helmets. Suddenly the destroyers from farther out opened up on the beach wire and obstacles. The whooshing shells landed with dull thuds in the sand, and great columns of shell, wire, and concrete fragments rose into the air in slow motion. All but two or three panic-stricken surfers paddled quickly away from the approaching landing craft. The Japanese planners had not counted on the early south swell, and several of the landing craft began to plane on the crest of the waves, some sliding obliquely, but several going "over the falls" amidst the screams of the heavily laden Japanese, who realized they were about to die by drowning before they ever touched the shores of O'ahu. Soon the beach and waters along it were littered with pieces of equipment and bodies, but many soldiers went straight to the bottom with seventy pounds of gear strapped to their backs.

The majority of the troops from the Second Division, however, struggled ashore, squat men in drab, soaked uniforms, with webbed helmets and split-toed boots, their rifles with bayonets taller than they were, and their sword-wielding officers shouting orders and forming the troops into units on the Mā'ili beachhead. Shore resistance fire was sporadic, a slow, steady background of mortar and machine gun fire, and an occasional grenade flash. The seven weeks of almost daily air attacks on American positions had done their work.

The Twenty-fourth Infantry Division, based at Schofield Barracks, had responsibility for manning the coastal defenses from 'Ewa around the north shore to Kahuku, while her sister 25th had the same responsibility for the south shore from Kahuku to 'Ewa. Seven weeks of watching and waiting had led to the deployment of half the force along the coast and the other half on call at Schofield. With the invasion now clearly under way, the Schofield-based light infantry units moved quickly down through the narrow, winding Kolekole Pass, while armored units came the longer way along Kunia Road and

Kamehameha Highway.

At the same time, another scenario was playing itself out along the eight-mile strand of beach from Kailua to Waimānalo, with bathers and beachgoers shocked into the realization that the nightmare sword hanging over their heads had finally fallen. The Japanese landing on the eastern shore of Oʻahu, coming directly out of the rising sun, had crossed the mirrorlike blue waters and beached on the long, sloping shoreline, with the landing troops not even getting their boots wet. Shore resistance was also feeble from the weeks of aerial pounding by the Imperial Japanese Air Force.

American units contained the Japanese landing along the Waiʻanae Coast after reinforcements arrived, due in part to the narrow strip of land between the shore and the Waiʻanae Mountains, and the short, five-mile beach, but on the windward side, it was another matter. The much broader flat lands bordering the eight-mile-long shore, four miles wide in places, allowed the invading forces to wheel around the American defenders, driving them up the coast toward the Kāneʻohe Naval Air Station. The quiet little beach town of Kailua was witness to the relentless advance of Japanese forces pursuing the retreating American defenders. Behind the foot soldiers came the trucks, light tanks, and logistical support.

Kāneʻohe Naval Air Station was situated on the Mōkapu Peninsula, connected to the shore by a narrow road strand; the remainder of the neck of land was a marshy wetland. During the December 7 attack, the Air Station was practically defenseless, its guns and ammo locked up securely. Since then, however, the defenders had hurriedly constructed a series of concrete bunkers on the far side of the ponds, reef, and swampland. Now retreating American troops withdrew behind this miniature Bataan Peninsula and waited for the attackers.

Three days after the Māʻili and Kailua landings, the main invasion force of the Fifth and Sixth divisions, forty-five thousand men, stormed ashore along the fifteen-mile coast of the

North Shore of Oʻahu, from Mokulēʻia to Kahuku. The defending American troops of the Twenty-fourth and Twenty-fifth divisions had been effectively drawn down and dispersed from the central point of concentration at Schofield to the western and eastern flanks, and now the main invasion force of seasoned amphibious troops landed on the lightly defended north coast. The only advance warning was the heavy air attacks by the First Air Fleet and the naval bombardment by the destroyers offshore. The coastal 4-gun battery of 155-mm field guns at Kawailoa and the battery of four eight-inch-caliber railroad guns were taken out in this concentrated attack. The little plantation town of Haleʻiwa, with its quaint wooden storefronts and shops, was set ablaze and quickly consumed. The popular Haleiwa Hotel took a direct hit, and blew apart in an explosion of glass and splinters.

Seen from above, the massive Japanese force seemed to engulf the North Shore like a slowly moving brown tide, funneling in from the flanks to move inland over the five-mile-wide "saddle plain" between the Koʻolau and Waiʻanae mountain ranges, inexorably moving toward Pearl Harbor and Hickam Air Force Base, twenty-five miles away. The Schofield saddle formed a natural corridor toward the main American bases on the leeward side of Oʻahu. This classic Japanese maneuver had been used against American and Philippine forces, with the main seaborne landings at Lingayen Gulf on Luzon after landings in three other places that protected the flanks of the main invasion force. As in Singapore, the main coastal batteries along the Honolulu coast faced outward toward the sea. They offered no protection against invaders coming in the "back door." Meanwhile, small invading forces landed at the undefended cities on the outer islands—Hilo, Lahaina, Līhuʻe.

From the flanks of invading Japanese forces moving up the central plains of Oʻahu, Japanese soldiers on bicycles raced quickly up the numerous cane roads to encircle and cut off American defenders being pushed up the slope toward the town of Wahiawā and Schofield Barracks. General Yamashita had used this "hook tactic" of encirclement in his swift march four hundred miles down the Malay Peninsula toward the "impregnable" British Gibraltar of the Pacific, Singapore. With three major Japanese forces converging from three different directions on O'ahu, the stage was set for the final climactic struggles on all fronts.

VOICES

7
The Grandfather's Story, Part 3

We Japanese workers found ourselves suddenly stranded in little camps, like islands, in a sea of waving sugarcane. Although we were only a few hundred yards from the real ocean, sometimes it felt more like a desert, for we could see nothing of the blue water, like back home in my family village. Kahuku Plantation covered thousands of acres and employed hundreds of us—Hawaiians, Chinese, Japanese, and later Filipinos. We were given numbers—on bangos, little round metal tags—to replace our names. From long lines of workers, we were called by these numbers to get our pay. For a while we lost the feeling of who we were, and we had to build that again, first as human beings, then as Japanese, then as united workers. That took a long time, as I will tell you.

The hard work, that is what I remember the most: the sore backs, aching muscles, and callused hands. We knew nothing about growing sugarcane, but we soon learned more than we ever wanted to know. There were three main jobs in the fields— *hoe hana* (weeding), *hana wai* (irrigating), and *hāpai kō* (harvesting). Each was broken down into specific tasks—plowing, planting, ditching, stripping, cutting, carting, and so on—and each had its particular misery. When were at *hoe hana*, for example, we were marched out to the fields and set to work in long rows with the hoes to clear the weeds. We weren't allowed to straighten up; we just kept our backs bent into the hoeing. After hours of this, the pain in our shoulders and backs was never ending. Over us rode or stood the *luna*, or boss. He watched us constantly—"no talking," "move faster"—we had to keep bent over and keep moving in the rows through the newly planted cane stalks.

The sugarcane grew quickly in the hot sun and steady, gentle rains. Soon the cane stalks were ten or twelve feet high, thickly matted and overgrown at the base. Into this jungle we waded for the stripping of the dead leaves, and the cutting. For me, this was the worst job. In the middle of the fields of waving cane, it was incredibly hot and dusty. There was no air or breeze, and when we tried to breathe, the cane dust and red clay dirt filled our lungs and left us choking. Because the leaves had sharp spines and edges, we had to wear heavy pants, shirts, and gloves, so soon we were sweating, then covered with the dust, which looked like chocolate powder. The fields were full of wasps, yellow jackets, and other stinging and biting insects, and they did not like to have their nests and burrows disturbed. Still we had to keep moving in long rows, stripping or cutting the cane. The cut cane then had to be bundled and loaded into wagons (and then later, cane trains) and hauled to the big mill. Work at the mill itself had its own share of miseries. The mills were big factories in the fields, full of steam engines, mechanical presses, and giant boilers. There was continuous noise—a thunderous roar—and terrific heat from the steam engines, even at night. There was a night shift during the grinding season, no letup at all, until the tall cane was turned into a sticky syrup or white crystals.

Payday was twice a month, when we lined up in front of the manager's office and waited for our bango number to be called. Every time, we were disheartened when we opened our pay envelopes, for deductions had been made for our plantation store purchases, and behind us were the merchants, housekeepers, laundry ladies, and others we owed money to. At that time, we earned about fifteen dollars a month, so saving money was very slow and hard. It was easy to be discouraged when month after month passed in this back-breaking labor, and we had nothing saved, nothing to show for it, nothing to send home. Many times we found ourselves in debt the day after payday, going deeper in the hole. We heard of better jobs paying more money elsewhere, especially in town, but we had signed three-year labor contracts to work on the plantations. Some of my friends tried *ha'alele hana*—deserting, running away and breaking the contract. But the police and special gangs of men were always on the lookout for escapees; we were like prisoners, you know. Rewards of ten dollars were posted for runaways, and so my friends who tried it were always caught. Where can you hide on an island? When that happened, they were fined, then given more time on their contracts to work off—that's why it was called a "penal contract" system!

It was not an easy life on the plantations, especially in the early years, but to be honest about it, life was generally hard everywhere back then. I remember, in Japan, the backbreaking labor in the rice fields, in the mud and water under the hot sun. Then the tax collectors of the *daimyō* lords or Meiji government came around and took almost half of what we grew for taxes. Perhaps life was better on the plantations, for most of us stayed in Hawai'i, even when we had a chance to leave after our contracts were finished. And it was hard elsewhere. I had a Norwegian-American friend back then, Sven. He and I had gotten to know each other on the night shift at the mill. Sven and his family moved to the Great Plains of America in the same year I came to Hawai'i. He told me of his childhood in the Dakota Territory, where his father had 160 acres of land under the Homestead Act. He and his family lived in a house made of dirt or sod! We Japanese need to be clean, purified, with a bathhouse to scrub away the dirt and pollution. Where Sven grew up, water was very hard to come by. The pioneer life on the prairie, as it was called, was unbelievably hard. The broiling heat of the summers was replaced by the freezing cold and blizzards of the long winters—from 120 degrees in July to 80 degrees below zero in December! The land was hard and unyielding, with continual droughts and even plagues of grasshoppers that ate everything. His family finally gave up after seven years, and Sven moved on. He said life in Hawai'i on the plantations, hard as it was, was far better than the pioneer life on the Great Plains of America. And I think, for me, the dust of the cane fields was better than the mud of the Japanese rice paddies.

VISTAS

8
The Last Stands

I begin my lecture today with a passage from General Mori's battle order, which gives us an idea of the excitement and ferocity of the Japanese onslaught that overwhelmed the American forces in Hawai'i:

Imperial General Order 667

Victorious Soldiers of His Imperial Majesty, I bring you great news to stir you into even more heroic efforts. Yesterday, February 15, 1942, General A. E. Percival, Commander of British forces in Singapore, surrendered to Lt. General Tomoyuki Yamashita. The great Anglo-Saxon Gibraltar of the Pacific is now part of the Empire of the Rising Sun! In just seventy-three days, General Yamashita gallantly led his forces four hundred miles down the Malay Peninsula, flanking, encircling, and then defeating numerous British and Indian units, then assaulting Singapore Island itself, only a little smaller than O'ahu, which we now almost have in our grasp. The British force that surrendered was four times larger than the 25th Army of Japan; 130,000 British and Indian soldiers have lost their honor, their right to be called soldiers. Already General Yamashita is being hailed as "The Tiger of Malaya."

The Gods of War now smile upon us, my sons of the Rising Sun.

As Singapore was the British Gibraltar of the Pacific in the West, so Hawai'i is the American Gibraltar of the Pacific in the East, and soon it also shall be in our hands. I exhort you to make the final supreme effort on behalf of His Imperial Majesty and wrest these islands from the hands of the American invaders who so underhandedly stole them from the Hawaiian queen, and altered the natural destiny of these lands from being part of an Asian Empire, the empire of Japan!

(signed) Lt. General Hiro Mori

Behind the peninsular defenses of Mōkapu, the troops of the Twenty-fifth Infantry Division and the naval personnel from the Kāne'ohe Naval Air Station waited for the assault from the massing Japanese forces that had landed on the beaches of Kailua and Waimānalo and had driven the American defenders back to the peninsula, almost completely surrounded by water—the Pacific waters of Kāne'ohe Bay on three sides, and the saltwater marsh and ponds on the landward side. The bridge over the narrow road had been blown up, leaving three hundred yards of swampy marshland and sandbars for the invaders to cross.

The leading elements of the Seventh Division of the Imperial Japanese Army were contemptuous of the retreating Americans, who had hardly put up a fight to oppose their landings. The jubilant troops, who had hardly yet fired a shot or bloodied their bayonets, took matters into their own hands. With some of the junior officers in front, they formed themselves into squads and, with swords drawn and screams of "*Banzai*" on their lips, charged recklessly across the expanse of shallow marsh. Their yells were silenced by the hail of machine gun bullets and crashing mortar shells, which cut them down by the score. In anger and frustration at seeing their comrades so wantonly slaughtered, other waves spontaneously followed them into the jaws of death. Soon, hundreds of Imperial Army soldiers, and parts of soldiers, were left floating in the shallow lagoons or littering the sandbars. Overhead, the marsh birds floated and screeched, disturbed from their nests by the struggling troops and falling shells.

A similar fate met those troops attempting a seaborne landing on the northern edge of the peninsula near the airstrip. Soon, the bay was filled with floating corpses and sinking rafts and landing crafts, blown out of the water by mortar rounds and point-blank fire from the encased artillery. Wave after wave from these two principal approaches was repulsed by the dwindling number of defenders. Maintaining the defense perimeter around the Mōkapu Peninsula became increasingly difficult, as men raced back and forth to the invasion points. After three days and nights, the inevitable breakthrough occurred, near Pyramid Rock. The Japanese troops were by this time enraged at the losses inflicted by such a puny force, a loss of face that could only be removed by the summary executions of the surviving defenders. And so it was done, by rifle fire, by bayonet thrusts, and by beheadings with gleaming *samurai* swords. This ended resistance on the "little Bataan Peninsula," as it came to be called.

The main invading force surged up the saddle from the North Shore toward Pearl Harbor, some twenty-five miles away, spreading out through the fields of sugarcane. In their path lay Schofield Army Barracks, halfway to Pearl. Hidden pockets of defenders slowed the advance through the high cane fields, so three dozen light Japanese tanks lined up in front of the advancing troops, pressing down the cane stalks and clearing paths through the fields, routing defenders hidden in the positions. Whether by accident (a hot shell), or intent (a Zippo lighter), the cane field burst into flames. The men in the mini-tanks had no chance; the wall of fire was on them before they could get out or turn the tanks back toward the sea. In the crackling fire could be heard the screams of the tank crews being roasted alive. The tanks became ovens, and the small of burning flesh soon overpowered the sickly sweet smell of cane sugar and ripe pineapples.

Once the fire had burned itself out, the oncoming surge of troops resumed its march, through the smoldering fields and pall of black smoke. Further up on the slopes, above the cane fields, the yellow pineapples on their stalks resembled giant hand grenades, and men on both sides greedily slashed them open to slake their thirst. When shells or rifle fire hit them, they did in fact blow up like giant hand grenades, or they rose gracefully in a high arc and thudded on the ground like big duds.

Schofield Barracks, then America's largest military post, became the scene of fierce fighting as Japanese troops surged through Macomb Gates. American soldiers, loathe to lose their home base, resisted the Japanese forces building by building. The post theater, the fire station, the hospital, the stockade, and especially the quads, were contested bitterly. Heavy artillery pieces leveled the graceful art deco buildings one by one, until Schofield Barracks, once the pride of the U.S. Army, lay in smoking ruins. Nearby Wheeler Field suffered the same fate. As American forces retreated to the leeward side of the plateau, they blew up the bridges across the ravines to slow the Japanese advance. At this point, that was all they could do; the Japanese invasion force could not be stopped.

While a branch of the invading force veered west down through the Kolekole Pass to encircle American forces at Māʻili, the main flood continued unabated down the gentle slope toward leeward Oʻahu. Suddenly a great *"Banzai"* cheer went up among the troops as they first sighted the lochs of Pearl Harbor, the ruined superstructures of battleships, and the carrier *Enterprise*, straddling the entrance to the harbor. Advancing Japanese troops surged down Kunia Road toward Waiʻanae behind the American forces, and down Kamehameha Highway toward Pearl Harbor and Hickam Air Force Base. Meanwhile, frightened residents of Pearl City fled in panic, with what belongings they could carry, toward Honolulu.

American troops holding the line in Māʻili withdrew before they were flanked by Japanese forces coming down the Kolekole Pass. The advance forces had been spotted in time to pull back, but not in time to prevent their advance through the pass. The surviving remnants of the Twenty-fourth Division pulled back to Kahi Point, the narrowest point between the mountains and the sea. Here they made their last stand. They were now encircled by Japanese forces coming from the rear. Rather than lose more men in brutal frontal and rear assaults, Japanese commanders annihilated the defenders in their exposed positions with heavy artillery barrages. Japanese forces from the original landing now linked up with the main North Shore invasion force, and they moved on the remaining bases— Pearl, Hickam, and the Army Command Headquarters at Fort Shafter.

At all three military installations, the fighting was sporadic, much less intense than the defense of Schofield. Its loss seemed to have broken the back of American defense and resistance. There was of course fighting in and around the shipyard, hangers, and offices, but the end was never in doubt. Surviving American defenders—soldiers and civilian "minutemen," the Organized Defense volunteers, the Hawaiʻi Rifles, and thousands of others in home guard units—made their way through the downtown area, retreating before the advancing Japanese forces. The few surviving coastal guns of Fort DeRussy— Battery Randolph—and the array of high-caliber mortars inside Diamond Head at Fort Ruger did no good; these guns, like the artillery of Singapore, pointed out toward the sea. One by one, small knots of armed defenders throughout the city surrendered or were shot down, some shot even after they surrendered. General Delos Emmons perished in his underground command post at Āliamanu Crater. Admiral Chester Nimitz made an ill-fated escape attempt by PT boat to a waiting sub. General Douglas MacArthur had made a lucky getaway like this from Corregidor, but Nimitz's boat was spotted, strafed, and sunk in the Moloka'i Channel. The loss of Nimitz and Halsey was more serious than the loss of two carrier task forces, for they would have been the proponents of carrier-based air power.

The downtown area of Honolulu was largely untouched by the fighting as American and Hawaiian defenders fell back. Many civilians caught between the contending forces fled toward the mountains. A long-remembered holdout was the squad of U.S. Marines who seized Aloha Tower with a small arsenal of weapons. The marines held up the Japanese advance for several hours, accounting for scores of Japanese dead. Japanese commanders decided to make an example of these detestable *gaijin*, to demonstrate the overwhelming power of Imperial Japan.

The battleship *Nagato* was cruising offshore, providing coastal bombardment in advance and support of the invading forces. Now she was ordered to sail into Honolulu Harbor, threading her way between the abandoned ships—fishing trawlers, tugboats, and private yachts. The great 220-foot battleship stood directly off Aloha Tower and its defenders. The pings of their small-arms fire against the heavily armored side of the battleship brought howls of laughter and derision from the sailors aboard and the soldiers ashore, well under cover from the Aloha Tower marksmen. The forward sixteen-inch guns of the *Nagato* were lowered, at point-blank range, toward the top of Aloha Tower. Suddenly there was an explosion of orange flame and smoke from the big guns, and an explosion of concrete and stone from the Tower. When the smoke cleared, the top two floors of Aloha Tower, and the men it contained, were gone, obliterated.

The last stand of American forces took place on the Nu'uanu Pali Road lookout. Here, survivors of the Twenty-fifth Division took up positions on the breathtaking 1,400-foot cliffs overlooking the windward coast. The Pali Lookout was world-famous for its cool winds and dramatic waterfalls. The fluted green cliffs fell away in a sheer vertical drop. Here, in 1795,

Kamehameha the Great defeated the Hawaiian king of O'ahu, driving many of his defenders off the jagged cliffs. Here was the place where the Hawaiian Islands were joined together into a single kingdom under a single monarch. Almost exactly a hundred years later, the American annexationists seized the lands and built the army and navy bases across the islands. Here, now, on February 23, 1942, the last American defenders were overwhelmed. They held the pass for several days, preventing the invading windward forces from joining up across the Ko'olau Mountains. The three hundred defenders—surviving marines, navy, and army personnel—made their way up the Old Pali Road from the windward side, and dug themselves in behind the natural stone and lava parapets at the peak of the pass. They placed charges beneath the concrete shelving that supported the road where it jutted out over the Pali, and waited. The three leading Japanese troop transports plunged over the side when the charge was detonated, the men falling and bouncing off the side of the cliff like rag dolls. A narrow section of the road survived, and clung precariously to the side of the cliff—too narrow for a motorized vehicle, but wide enough for soldiers to pass single file—into the gun sights of the defenders. Dozens more valiant imperial troopers died that day and the next, trying to force the pass. With bazookas, mortars, light artillery, and rifles, the three hundred Americans held the Nu'uanu Pass. Japanese air attacks failed to dislodge them. Japanese artillery attacks also made little headway.

Now, with most of O'ahu under their control, Japanese troops advanced up Nu'uanu Valley from the Honolulu side. The cool, lush valley echoed to the sounds of Japanese troops marching quick-time up the Old Pali Road. The defenders were soon surrounded. The choice for the surviving defenders was stark and simple—throw themselves on the Japanese bayonets or throw themselves off the sheer cliff to the rocks below. Surrender meant almost certain death at the hands of the enraged Japanese soldiers, and so the last surviving free

American soldiers jumped, plunging hundreds of feet down the face of the cliff into the undergrowth below. Although none of the Americans had likely heard of Leonidas and the three hundred Spartans at Thermopylae in 480 B.C., holding the mountain pass against the invading Persians, they were in later years to be compared with them. In an eerie reenactment of the battle of Nu'uanu Pali in 1795, when Kamehameha the Great conquered Hawai'i, the islands now came under another monarch— Emperor Hirohito, his Imperial Majesty of Japan. The Greater East Asia Co-Prosperity Sphere now stretched almost six thousand miles, from the island of Singapore in the west to the island of O'ahu in the east. Hawai'i was now a forward base of the Japanese Empire's defense perimeter, and the United States was deprived of its major military springboard in the Pacific. The "hinge of history" now changed the trajectory of Hawai'i's future.

VOICES

9
The Grandfather's Story, Part 4

No one liked the hard work and low pay, but the two things that we plantation workers most resented were the lack of freedom—the controls on our lives—and the lack of dignity—being treated like an object, a thing, instead of a human being. The bosses had a long time to work out these things. The first sugar plantations in Hawai'i had been started almost fifty years before we Japanese arrived, so the managers and lunas had many tactics to handle us, at least in the beginning.

We lived our lives by the company rules—from "whistle to whistle," we used to say. At five a.m., the whistle blew to wake us up and get us moving. And we had to move fast. Pretty soon a "policeman" would come through the camps, pounding on doors, or even kicking them in to rouse slowpokes. We had to dress and eat fast, to gather for transport to the fields in wagons or the train. By six in the morning we were in the fields in gangs. They gave us a half hour for lunch between eleven-thirty and noon, then work under the midday sun until four-thirty. Usually there were gangs of twenty to thirty workers under one *luna* on horseback. If you were late, the luna yelled, "You *pohō*"—out of luck. That meant your pay was docked or you were fined. Sometimes the lunas used the whips they carried, but most often they kicked or slapped or cursed the worker who didn't do things right, or "by the rules."

Pau hana was at four-thirty, but we didn't get back to the barracks until after five, usually so tired we couldn't do much of anything. But we had only three hours after that to bathe, write letters, and talk story before "lights out" at eight-thirty, again by the whistle or siren. Soon it was early morning again, and the routine repeated itself day after day, month after month, year after year. Every plantation camp had its list of rules—rules about cleanliness, rules about no gambling, rules about not leaving camp without permission, rules about everything—as if we were bad little children! The managers were like our fathers, and sometimes we had good managers, and sometimes bad managers. It was all up to them. Sometimes a manager would take a special interest in a worker and his family, if, say, the worker was a good baseball player or had a talent as a mechanic, but it was not the normal treatment. It was expected that if you wanted better treatment, you better have a gift for the boss too, at Christmas or for his birthday. The bosses of course were all white—haoles from America—and the lunas were Portuguese. Most of the skilled mechanic or engineering or office jobs were filled with Scottish or Norwegian men. There was no chance to move up, no matter how skilled or hard-working you were, if you were Japanese.

I mentioned that we Japanese lived in different camps from the Chinese, Hawaiian, or Filipino workers. In a way, that was natural, because we liked to be with our countrymen who shared the same values and interests, and ate the same food. But the bosses used that against us too. We were paid different wages for the same work, depending on our nationality. Hawaiians and all haoles got more money than we Japanese for the same jobs, and the Chinese and Filipinos got paid less for the same work. And everyone got paid better than the women workers. That made everyone envious of the group above them, and scornful of the groups below them. Lots of fights started over this. The bosses promoted competition between the groups also. Absentee lists were posted by nationality, and we Japanese were reminded that we were better treated than the newly arriving workers from the Philippines. The bosses encouraged us to have "race pride" and not to be outdone by another group. Baseball teams were organized by race—Japanese versus Hawaiian, Chinese versus Filipino, and so on. Looking back, it was a clever way of keeping us divided, and it worked for a long time. The plantations began to give us things to make life better—a baseball field, a movie theater, running water—but it was also a way to make us more dependent, more under their control, because what can be given can be taken away!

The planters used representatives of our home governments to keep us in line and inspire us to work harder. Occasionally the Japanese consul in Honolulu would come around and give us a speech, imploring us Japanese to do nothing that would bring shame upon our country or our families. The planters set up a Central Japanese League to promote mutual obligations and settle disputes between workers and the company. It seemed as if no one was on our side, except other workers. Over time though, a community feeling developed, first among the Japanese themselves. We came from different parts of Japan, different villages, but in Hawai'i those things didn't matter. We learned to talk with the other groups—Hawaiian, Chinese, Filipino—through "pidgin," and we discovered we had many things in common, such as how we were treated by the company doctors.

Being sick usually didn't keep you out of the cane fields, because the company doctor had to certify you were really sick. You needed a paper from him to stay in bed, and he usually wasn't willing to give you one unless you were really bad off. Complaints and symptoms were often ignored, and you were sent back to the fields. The so-called "hospital" was like a jail, and the "medicines" were even worse. It was better to rely on traditional herbs and cures, and just pray to the Compassionate Buddha not to get sick. What we Japanese experienced on the plantations was true, I think, for the thousands of workers from Hawai'i, China, and the Philippines. The plantation was where we became the people of Hawai'i. It was our "melting pot."

VISTAS

10
The Rising Sun in Hawai'i

I begin my lecture today with a common speech given to American prisoners assembled on the 'Ewa plains. It gives you some idea of the ordeal they were about to face.

"The emperor has given you your lives. You have disgraced yourselves as soldiers by surrendering, by remaining alive instead of dying gloriously as warriors for your country. The day of your country, America, is over in the Pacific and Asia. This is true for all Anglo-Saxon countries. The century of shame and humiliation you have heaped on the peoples of Asia shall be repaid to you many times over! Even though you are just lowly prisoners, you are eternal enemies of Japan. You must promptly obey every order of every Japanese. If you do not, you will just as promptly forfeit your miserable lives that are so important to you. Obey, work, and you might live. The peace-loving imperial forces will not inflict harm on those who are obedient, but those who violate the Japanese spirit will have cause to regret it."

The American prisoners from the various battles and skirmishes around O'ahu were gathered together on the dusty plains of 'Ewa. Dozens, then hundreds of hollow-eyed men were stripped, then trussed with rope or wire tied around their wrists from behind and looped around their necks so that struggle meant strangulation. Around certain, unlucky knots of prisoners, the grinning, growling guards gathered, with rocks, ax handles, and rifle butts. They methodically and mercilessly beat the men senseless.

As the number of prisoners grew into the several hundreds, they were moved into a field ringed with barbed wire, the guards armed with machine guns. The midday sun blazed; there was no shade, no water. Supplications for water or moans from the wounded only brought savage beatings from the abusive, smirking guards. All day long, and through the night, the prisoners were gathered. At night the suffering from the dry heat was replaced with the cold dampness and chilling wind off the ocean. The meager possessions—watches, wallets, pens, medals, rings—were confiscated and fought over by the idle soldiers as the miserable groups of prisoners were brought in. Any prisoner with a Japanese trophy of war—coins, flag, knife—was immediately dragged forward before the prisoners and beheaded.

On the morning of the second day, the number of prisoners being brought to the site dwindled, and the Japanese officers barked orders to get the men on their feet and remove the wires and ropes with which they had been hog-tied. Now began the "death march" of the more than twenty-thousand prisoners to the Diamond Head Prison Camp. Many of the men had already been force-marched to this location, some from Fort Shafter on the outskirts of Honolulu. Now they had to turn around and march back the way they had come. The prisoners were formed up in long lines, four or five abreast, with armed soldiers on either side. The same procedure was being repeated on the windward side, the difference being that the intense heat was replaced with the long steep climb up the Pali Road. On both of these forced marches, stragglers were summarily killed—

clubbed, bayoneted, or shot where they had collapsed. For amusement, several prisoners were pushed screaming over the edge of the Pali road as it climbed hundreds of feet into the clouds.

As new units of Japanese soldiers joined this miserable parade, they made up for having missed the initial beatings by inflicting their own. Individual prisoners, or small groups, were pulled out of line and forced to run gauntlets of soldiers armed with bamboo poles or two-by-fours. Those who fell rarely got up, being ganged up upon and beaten to a pulp. Occasionally an officer would restore discipline and end the torture, but this was rare. More often, they just laughed at the ingenuity of the punishments, or joined in.

As the long columns of prisoners straggled through the streets of Pearl City, groups of the remaining civilians gathered along the street in silence. At first, a few good samaritans made efforts to give water to the men half-crazed with thirst. The charity was met with savage reprisals; soldiers clubbed them to the ground and often to death with rifle butts. Survivors later reported that on occasion, a few unlucky souls trying to help prisoners were set on fire. This happened primarily to Filipino men and women trying to *kōkua* the prisoners. The same thing was happening on a much greater scale on the island of Luzon, as American prisoners were force-marched from the Bataan Peninsula to Camp O'Donnell.

As the front end of the five-mile-long string of prisoners entered Honolulu through Iwilei and Chinatown, the crowds of people along the streets grew larger. Men, women, and children stood in silence as the beaten American soldiers passed by, some with hands over their hearts, some with hands clasped in prayer. An occasional shock of recognition, of a friend, of a relative, of a lover, would elicit a cry of grief or pain. This usually brought a savage act of violence against both the prisoner and his acquaintance. Soon the scenes of recognition were replaced with quiet sobbing.

Kalākaua Avenue was the proud gateway to Waikīkī—the

"playground of the Pacific." It had witnessed many parades in honor of its royalty and mainland celebrities—beautiful *pāʻū* riders in their long silk gowns, flower-bedecked floats and lines of smartly dressed army, navy, and marine troops, Boy Scouts, clowns, and hula dancers. This day, however, Waikīkī witnessed a parade unlike any other—sixteen thousand haggard, gaunt, and hollow-eyed men, naked, barefoot, or in rags, stumbling along, their eyes fixed on their bloody feet. Behind them came the new contingents of Japanese troops who had not been part of the invading force. They were disembarking from troopships pulling into Honolulu Harbor. Their baggy uniforms were yet clean, not covered by the red dirt of the cane and pine fields that marked their brethren already baptized by battle.

Looming up over Waikīkī was Diamond Head—the volcanic crater that had become the trademark, the most familiar landmark of Hawaiʻi on the travel posters, the first recognizable sight for the cruiseliner tourists as they rounded the bend of the island. The summit of Diamond Head projected 760 feet into the air on the ocean side—a majestic profile in daylight, but especially by moonlight from the hotels and beaches of Waikīkī. On this day, it poured forth black smoke from its severely cratered face. This had been the site of the Lēʻahi Observation Station—the big-gun sighting and targeting post for the leeward coastal forts. Despite its concealed location, being built into the wall of the crater for the Coast Artillery in 1911, the multileveled concrete structure had been itself targeted by Japanese naval guns and reduced to a smoking ruin.

On the mountain, or *mauka,* side of Diamond Head crater, the prisoners passed through a narrow tunnel into the floor of the long-extinct tuff cone, an area of 475 acres containing the shattered remnants of the coastal mortar batteries. The dry brown walls of the crater rose sharply all around the prisoners as they were herded into the far corner. The sunlight was brilliantly reflected into their eyes from all directions once the choking brown dust settled—onto the prisoners and into their lungs, adding unmercifully to their agony of thirst. A barbed wire enclosure, surrounded by rickety machine gun towers, had been hastily erected on fifty acres of the Waikīkī side of the crater wall. Later nicknamed "The Frying Pan," this little corner of hell was going to be their home for the next three years, at least for the two out of three soldiers who survived the ordeal of being the prisoners of the Imperial Japanese Army. In time, the number of prisoners grew smaller, as the number of dusty graves topped by wooden crosses grew larger.

Back in Waikīkī, another horrific drama was taking place. Behind the strand of glistening white sand beach, the three great hotels dominated the scene. On the far side of Kalākaua Avenue stretched the "Jungle"—street after street of low-rise beach bungalows and cottages, the vacation homes of the less well-to-do Hawai'i tourists. These quaint wooden structures, with small palm trees or banana patches out front, had been designated "Camp Yamamoto," after the architect of this great Japanese victory over America. They were to be immediately occupied by the front-line assault forces in the invasion of O'ahu, as a reward for their heroic efforts.

Cowering within the cottages and bungalows were the terrified guests, tourists from California, New Jersey, and dozens of other American states who had been unlucky enough to visit the islands before December 7, and who now found themselves caught in the coils of fate. The weary, angry Japanese soldiers burst through the doors of their assigned quarters. If the doors were bolted or locked, they furiously kicked them in or smashed the glass with their rifle butts. The men were beaten, stabbed, kicked, bayoneted, or shot, depending on the whim of the men with guns. The women suffered a more agonizing ordeal. The screams of the ravaged women mixed with the laughter of the soldiers participating in the gang rapes. Naked women, hysterical and bloody, raced into the streets after a while, only to be grabbed by the hair by newly arriving troops and dragged back screaming into the rooms. The little wooden houses, which had been the scenes of so many wonderful memories over the years—romantic trysts, passionate honeymoons, wild parties—became places of horror and dread in the scarred memories of the survivors.

The great ladies of Waikīkī Beach—the Halekūlani, Royal Hawaiian, and Moana hotels—became the billets of the Japanese officers for the time being. The pink, Spanish art-deco–style Royal Hawaiian became the home of the Imperial Japanese Army officer corps, while the white, Victorian Moana soon filled with Combined Fleet naval officers. Air Force officers and pilots moved into the stately Hālekulani. Although the officers were better behaved than the enlisted men in the "Jungle," they didn't hesitate to confiscate the belongings of the well-heeled guests. Those who protested were quickly dispatched with pistols. The others were driven into the street with nothing more than the shirts or dresses they happened to be wearing. They were of course considered to be the parasites and the bloated, decadent oppressors of the poor of the world—in Asia, Africa, and the Middle East, as well as America. It was they who turned proud Japanese immigrants into coolies and gardeners in California, and now it was their turn to suffer. Inside, the sound of broken glass and crashing chandeliers mixed with Japanese marching songs as the officers found whiskey bottles behind the inlaid wooden bars. Soon, drunken officers and their men waded into the gentle surf of Waikīkī Beach and fell down laughing and then unconscious in the moonlit sand. And so ended the first night of Japanese occupation in Hawai'i—the first of more than fourteen hundred days for the people of Hawai'i.

VOICES

11
The Grandfather's Story, Part 5

By the year 1893, after almost ten years of working on the plantation, I began to realize that I would never save enough money to help my family in Japan redeem their land, and consequently that I would probably end my days here in Hawai'i. I was now twenty-five years old, and still unmarried, living in the bachelors' barracks. I resolved to marry and begin a family—to continue my family line, to enjoy something of the pleasures of this world, to leave something behind. Since women from Japan of my age were few in Hawai'i, I turned to a matchmaker for an arranged marriage with a suitable girl from Japan. In this way, I exchanged letters and pictures with Etsuko, and she became my "picture bride" wife.

I received permission from my plantation *luna* for a week off to meet her ship, and so I happened to be in Honolulu when the planters overthrew the queen, the sister of King Kalākaua. She had been on the throne for two years, since the sad death of her brother. I think the king died of a broken heart after the businessmen took away his power two years after I came to Hawai'i. They forced on him a new constitution—a "bayonet constitution" it was called, which put the businessmen in the cabinet and important government jobs. King Kalākaua became a puppet, just as the emperors were for the shoguns, or military warlords, who ruled Japan. The new *bakufu*, or "tent government," was located on Merchant Street, the center of the Big Five headquarters. The new queen, Liliʻuokalani, was determined to restore the monarchy and the Hawaiian people to their rightful positions with a new constitution she had written, and for this, she was overthrown. In this takeover, the businessmen were aided by the United States. American marines patrolled the streets in a show of force, while Hawaiians wept openly. Later, the queen was arrested and imprisoned in the palace itself for plotting to regain what was rightfully hers, since the American government was going to do nothing to help her.

My country was greatly upset by this overthrow, and the emperor sent the warship *Naniwa*, commanded by Captain Heihachiro Togo, to Hawaiʻi to protect us Japanese in Hawaiʻi, for the businessmen justified their actions partly by claiming they acted to prevent Japan from seizing Hawaiʻi. Five years later, in 1898, the American government used the same excuse for annexing Hawaiʻi. We *issei*, or first generation immigrants, made up almost half the island's population by that time, but it was never the intention of Japan to swallow the islands, as the Americans did. My country's government refused to recognize the new Provisional Government and the "Republic" of Hawaiʻi in 1893, but it did no good. We could not stop the United States. But Japan under the Meiji emperor grew stronger, and defeated China the next year, then the Russian Empire ten years later. My heart was full of pride! Russia had become the dominant Western power in North Asia, but she was humbled by little Japan.

To return to my story, my new wife arrived at a time of great sorrow and change. She became a dutiful wife, fixing my meals, washing my clothes, working in the fields, and later giving me a son. Because I was now married, we could move into a small cottage we shared with another young couple, and in 1905, my son, Togo, was born. But conditions were still hard, and getting harder. Prices were going up, but not our pay. Many of my generation had decided to stay in Hawai'i, so we had built many Buddhist temples, Shinto shrines, and Japanese language schools to teach our children the Japanese ways, and we had to support these. We were emboldened also with the changes that came with American annexation, for in 1900, when Hawai'i became part of America, the labor contract system could not be used under the American Constitution—it was like slavery!

Many of my fellow Japanese workers left the plantation at this time, returning to Japan or moving to California. (The businessman legislature even passed a law in 1907 to prohibit Japanese from moving from Hawai'i to the mainland.) Most of us stayed, though we made demands. We wanted Japanese overseers, a reduction of hours, and increased wages. Some workers, after they paid their bills, had less than three dollars a month to show for their hard labor in the fields. There was a growing spirit of *yamato damashī*, or solidarity, among us, and under the leadership of Japanese newspapermen, lawyers, and merchants in Honolulu, we formed the Japanese Higher Wages Association. In 1895, the planters and businessmen had formed the Hawai'i Sugar Planters Association to fight us. They set up a bonus system and long-term contracts to confuse us—no fixed wages, but different for each worker—but we were not fooled. A showdown was coming!

The Great 1909 Strike began on the 'Aiea plantation, but quickly spread to the Waipahu plantation, then our plantation in May. Soon there were eight thousand of us out together. There had been small labor actions on the plantations before, but now we were all together. Our major demand was, as our union's name suggested, for better, equal pay—from eighteen dollars a month to twenty-two fifty, the same as for other nationalities. All the plantations worked together against us; "make no concessions" was their slogan. They would not sit down and bargain with our union. Instead, they took actions against us. Strikers and their families received eviction notices from company houses; we had twenty-four hours to clear out. Together with our families, we made the long fifty-mile walk to Honolulu, where we lived in tents in ‘A‘ala Park. We received support from the large Japanese community in Honolulu, and from our union. They fed us in rice kitchens set up in the park, around the long "*kaukau* tables."

Meanwhile, the planters increased their attacks. Our strike and union leaders, Makino, Soga, and Tasaka, were arrested for "conspiracy." They were of course found guilty, and sentenced to ten months in jail. The police banned public speeches, and the National Guard was brought in to scare us. Most effectively, though, the planters brought in strikebreakers from different groups—Chinese, Portuguese, Hawaiian—to take our jobs. And then they began to import thousands of new workers from the Philippines, to weaken the Japanese labor strength on the plantations. After four months of this, we could hold out no longer, and the strike was called off. That was a sad day.

We were bitter and resentful at our treatment, and the non-Japanese community was fearful of us; the strike was presented as part of a Japanese conspiracy to take over the islands for Japan. That was not true of course; we only wanted equal treatment with other groups, and a living wage. And also dignity. We learned a lesson from this strike of 1909—that we Japanese alone were not enough; all of us on the plantations had to work together next time. And there would be a next time. Three months after the strike, after the planters had broken our union, they gave us equal wages, our main demand, and pardoned our leaders. They wanted to show us that they were generous victors, hoping to lessen our discontent. We held a big parade to celebrate, but we would remember.

I conclude my story in 1912. This was the year the Emperor Meiji died. He had come to the imperial throne in 1868, the year I was born. In his lifetime, and my own, Japan had changed from a closed, backward nation of feudal lords to a great world power, capable of defeating the Russian Empire. He had made Japan strong and rich. In the same time, in my lifetime, and with my labor, I did the same in Hawai'i. With my muscles and sweat, and that of my fellow workers from Japan, I helped build Hawai'i.

VISTAS

12
Despair . . . and Hope

I want to continue today with the fate of the American POWs. Their situation is clear from the standard speech given to new prisoners:

"American Prisoners—the emperor has given you your miserable lives; be grateful for that. You forfeited your chance to die honorably for your President, and now he has abandoned you to your fates. You are prisoners—the lowest of the low. Expect to be cold, expect to be hot. If you get sick, expect to die—that is the way of things. You have the hope of happiness in Heaven; do not expect to find it here. If you work, you will be kept alive. If you do not work, or cannot work, expect to die. You must also obey every order given you by the Japanese, any Japanese. Failure to obey quickly will mean severe punishment. If you are punished once, you will remember these words."

The dusty, parched bowl of Diamond Head Crater became the home of over thirty thousand American prisoners of war for the next three years. For almost ten thousand of these men, it also became their final resting place. While for German POW camps, the death rate for American prisoners was about one in twenty-five, for the Japanese camps in Asia and the Pacific, it was one in three. Japan never ratified the Geneva Convention on treatment of prisoners, and this grisly death rate was one of the results. The few acres inside the crater set aside for the prisoners was ringed with barbed wire and surrounded by sadistic guards with machine guns. They took out their anger and humiliation—over being stuck inside this dry, ugly crater while their comrades frolicked in the surf in their free time—by brutalizing the prisoners. Selection for judo practice was a favorite pastime. The unfortunate chosen prisoners would be kicked or thrown to the ground repeatedly by a team of guards. Failure to stagger to your feet immediately would result in a savage round of kicks by the guards in their heavy boots. On occasion, guards high up on the interior slopes of the crater would fire into the ranks of massed prisoners, and men would scatter in all directions, but with nowhere to hide.

The camp was nicknamed "The Frying Pan," with good reason. The hot sun shone down directly on the men from early morning, when it breached the crater rim, until later afternoon, when it finally sank below the western edge of the crater. The sunsets off Diamond Head are some of the most beautiful in the world, but these men did not see them. During the heat of midday, the sun's heat radiated back from the crater walls, and continued to do so long after the sun had set. The crater slopes upward over seven hundred feet on the seaward side, and this cut off the flow of both the cooling trade winds from over the Ko'olau Mountains in the daytime, and the gentle offshore breezes of the evening. The milling of thousands of prisoners and the occasional gusts of hot wind stirred up an enormous, almost permanent cloud of brown dust, which burned the eyes and choked the lungs. Many men went around with red bandannas always covering their mouths. In the winter months, the sometimes heavy rains turned the crater floor into an ankle-deep mud bowl, and the slow, soaking rains left everyone damp and chilled.

The main food was a watery rice gruel, with an occasional radish or bit of old fish floating about. Japanese soldiers often subsisted on very thin fare, and the POWs were given even less. On average the POW diet was about sixty percent less then the standard American military rations. This, coupled with heavy work requirements, meant malnutrition and slow starvation. The "work or die" policy compounded things. As the death rate in the camp approached twenty prisoners a day, selected prisoners were allowed to become beachcombers for dead fish, sea slugs, seaweed, spiny urchins—anything remotely edible. Prisoners at many of the work sites, such as at the Kawainui Marsh rice reclamation project, found freshwater crayfish or birds' eggs. Other prisoners were slipped food by their former local friends and neighbors. Other contraband—sugarcane stalks and cigarettes—were smuggled back into the camp, especially after the guards grew lax with the body searches. There was a sugar and nicotine obsession, and both commodities were valuable mediums of exchange—the camp's "currency." The other priceless commodity was salt, crudely processed from ocean water.

The two biggest problems, after the shortage of food, were water and sanitation. During the first year, prisoners filled several large tanks from the Waikīkī duck ponds by hand and dragged them back to the crater. The water was sometimes foul and brackish, especially in the drier summer. There were always long lines at the water taps. Eventually a water line was built and run into the camp, providing reasonably clean drinking water, but it was too late for several hundred prisoners who died of dysentery from the dirty duck pond water. The stench of the latrines also grew worse as that area grew in size. Dozens of men could be seen at any one time squatting over the slit trenches, bloody lavalavas pulled high around their waists.

The men had been allowed to go out in teams and collect palm fronds to construct shelters and lean-tos, and from a distance, a great distance, the POW camp looked like a quaint Polynesian village. Closer inspection revealed ragged lines of poorly built huts and "barracks," with the mess hall in one corner and the sick bay in another. To call these a "dining hall" or "hospital" was a misnomer; there was little to "dine" on in one case, and even fewer medicines and medical supplies in the other. The men in the sick bay were just slightly thinner than the men in the mess hall. All were hollow-eyed and gaunt, burned black and blistered from the ever-present sun. The blue sky overhead was rarely clouded over; this was the lure of Hawai'i, together with miles of beautiful beaches. Now the sky often drove men crazy with its changeless blueness.

Upon capture, the officers had been separated out and interned in the clearly better facilities on Sand Island, once the site of the labor immigration station for the contract sugar plantation workers from China, then Japan and the Philippines. The officers did not have to go out on work details—crushing coral for runways, clearing vegetation for planting, digging tunnels for highways. They were scorned for their better treatment, and blamed for the men's imprisonment. Being cut off from their officers and leaders, the men formed little "tribes" of four to six men, based on the state they were from or the job they held—little societies for mutual support and protection. If one of the group was sick, the others would cover for him—do his work, give him extra food, and nurse him back to health. A man without a group was a man waiting to die.

The support bands provided a decentralized order and discipline in the absence of the officers and military structure. The other discipline was of course provided by the Japanese. Starting with *tenkō*, or roll call, at six every morning, the guards divided up the men for the work details. The Americans were forced to sign a nonescape oath. Recaptured prisoners were tortured and killed in front of all the men. The Japanese also used group responsibility and group punishment; all in the group were made to pay for the mistakes and misbehavior of one. Forcing prisoners to run gauntlets of screaming guards armed with bamboo poles was a favorite punishment—it gave the guards a chance to work off their hatreds of the Americans. There was hatred on both sides, an incomprehension and repulsion that transcended any other conflict in modern history. There was a Brotherhood of the Captives versus the Army of the Captors!

The most feared and terrible punishment was the *chōmansai*—extreme overload. Batches of recalcitrant prisoners or victims of group punishment were hauled off to the damp and dark holds of the rusting hulks that had once been the American Pacific Fleet. These holds were used now as makeshift prisons for the "violators of the Japanese spirit." Hundreds of men were packed tightly together, with little water, air, or sunlight, for weeks at a time. In the summer, temperatures reached 120 degrees. At night, the cold ocean water outside created a chilly, damp icebox. The shivering men huddled together at night for body warmth, and went mad in the daytime with thirst and heat. Death by dehydration was the most common form of escape. By a sad and tragic irony, many of the men found themselves prisoners in the holds of the very ships they had once proudly served. The men nicknamed this treatment the "Oven"—out of the Frying Pan and into the Oven!

VOICES

13
Togo's Story, Part 1

I was born in 1905, the year of the great Japanese naval victory of Tsushima by Admiral Togo over the Russian fleet. My father gave me the nickname of "Togo," and that is what I came to be called. I spent my childhood on the Kahuku plantation, in the Japanese camp. My earliest memories are of my mother, and her exhausting work. After a day in the field hoeing cane, she did laundry, sewed clothes, and prepared meals for the single men later into the night. I remember the pained, tired, but determined look on her face. I grew up enjoying the plantation camp's amusements and pastimes. These included baseball and fishing, watching the cockfights and the older men gambling. It was not an unhappy childhood. There was a small library in the rec hall, and after I learned to read, I often buried my head in a book. School for us plantation kids was from seven in the morning until noon. This was so we could put in an afternoon's work when we were old enough, at age twelve. So I had some experience as a blacksmith's helper, a cane cutter, and a mill hand. I carried seventy-five-pound bundles of cane into the mill from the wagons before I was a teenager.

Since I was not born in the old country, my parents made sure I learned the values and culture of Japan. I attended Japanese language school and the Buddhist temple. The family was the center of my world, the center of my sense of self. At my father's knee, I learned to respect and honor my long line of ancestors—the grandfather and grandmother in Japan I had never known, and their parents before them. I must work hard, uphold the family name, and never bring shame upon it. I have a heavy obligation for the sacrifices they have made for me. I must remember my place in the order of things, and show obedience and piety to their "wishes." I remember too the Kenjin Kai—the Ken Club picnics—where all the families from the same prefectures in Japan got together for a day of friendship and gossip—fish cooking on the hibachis, shave ice and summer games. My parents spoke Japanese in a Hawai'i dialect, but we kids more often used pidgin, for I often played with Hawaiian and Filipino children growing up. Already my world was wider than that of my parents.

I probably would have remained a *nisei*, or second-generation, plantation worker with just an eighth-grade education had it not been for the Great Plantation Strike of 1920. The Great War of 1914 to 1918 had made Japan an ally of England and America, but it did not have a big effect in the islands, except for rising costs and prices, far ahead of wages. Again Japanese workers organized, this time on all islands—labor federations on O'ahu, Maui, Kaua'i, and the Big Island. These were joined together to form the Japanese Federation of Labor. By the time of the 1920 strike, the Filipino workers outnumbered the Japanese workers on the plantations, because the planters, determined to prevent another labor threat from the Japanese, recruited workers in the Philippines after the strike of 1909. The Filipino workers soon discovered the planters' promises were not to be trusted; they experienced the same conditions as other workers—low wages, poor housing, cruel lunas, and a lack of dignity. They formed their own Filipino Federation of Labor (FFL) under Pablo Manlapit. When he suddenly led the FFL out on strike in 1920, he urged our union to join them, and we voted to do so.

Our joint demands were for an eight-hour work day, paid maternity leave, an end to the bonus system, which tied us to the planters' "generosity," and a raise in pay from seventy-seven cents a day to three dollars a day. Soon eight thousand Filipino and Japanese workers were out on strike together! This time some of our own Japanese town leaders were against the strike, including the Japanese consul and the editor of *Hawaii Shimpo*, who we learned later was a paid stool pigeon, or spy, for the planters. The Sugar Planters Association—the bosses' union—tried to present the strike as a racial struggle between "loyal Americans" and the "foreign Japanese" over who would control the islands. Again, lurking in the background was a fear of Japan, now with an empire that included Formosa, Korea, and the Micronesian Mandated Islands. We were described in the major *haole* newspapers as an "alien race," led by "alien agitators"—Buddhist priests and newspaper writers. Again there were the evictions from the company houses, and the long trek from Kahuku down the windward coast and over the Pali to Honolulu, and tent camps in Kalihi where Japanese and Filipino families shared and struggled together.

The situation was complicated when Manlapit suddenly took the Filipino union out of the strike, then rejoined it amidst confusing rumors of bribery and payoffs to Manlapit. Arrests and strikebreakers and labor spies again became part of the arsenal of attack against us. Father, despite his age, was a strike leader, and this made him a marked man for the blacklist. What finally broke him, though, was the death of my mother at this time. The great Spanish influenza pandemic broke out during the Great War, killing twenty million people worldwide—twice the number of the Great War itself. It hit Hawai'i during the strike, when we were weakened by the struggle, living in tents and subsisting on a poor diet during the cold rainy season. Over two thousand people in Hawai'i came down with the flu, and 150 died, including my mother.

The strike lasted six long months, and in the end, it was broken by the planters. Three months later, the planters raised plantation worker pay by fifty percent, but only on their own terms; they would not bargain with a union. We learned another lesson—that we need to work together in the same union, all races and ethnic groups. This was the message being spread in America by the Industrial Workers of the World (IWW), broken by the federal government in the Great War. Because my father was blacklisted on the plantations for his role in the strike, and my mother was gone, we chose to remain in Honolulu. There my new life began.

VIGNETTES

14
The Savior of Kalaupapa

"Dear Lord, we pray to you today from the desolate shore where so many of your children perished from the *ma'i Pākē* of years past. Today we are like your children of Israel who exchanged bondage in Egypt for the desert wilderness of Sinai, to wander the cruel land without hope of sustenance, until You took mercy upon them, and gave them *mana* from Heaven. Help us, O God, to revive our faith, to endure the test of our spirits. Have mercy upon these children of Thy servants who came here in years past and lifted up a benighted people from the darkness of their lives, from their pagan practices—from human sacrifice, from cannibalism and infanticide, from worshipping the false gods of Polynesia. From all of these things did Your Chosen Messengers deliver us! Now their children need Your help. Please give me the strength to be Your Instrument, and together we will come through this test with our Faith renewed in Your everlasting mercy. Amen."

- prayer by William Kamaka at Kalaupapa

Messages passed to the prisoners from secret radios gave scant cause for hope, as the American war effort focused on

Europe. Instead of reports of rescue, wild rumors filled the void: that the war in Europe was over, that the fleet was coming, that they were going to be repatriated. Of course none of these predictions happened, and a mood of betrayal and abandonment would settle back onto the camp, until the next wild rumor sent hopes soaring for a little while. The Diamond Head Crater, which was their world, their prison, might as well have been on the dark side of the moon. The Hawaiian Islands are the most geographically isolated set of islands in the world, and never was this more deeply felt than by the American prisoners in the hands of the Japanese.

If there was any place more isolated and forlorn to American prisoners of the Japanese, it was the civilian internment camp on the Kalaupapa Peninsula on the island of Moloka'i. When the Japanese High Command learned of the relocation and internment of Japanese-Americans from the West Coast—over 110,000 American citizens removed and incarcerated—plans were made for a similar, smaller-scale version in Hawai'i. The Japanese could not have picked a more historically ironic site than the four-square-mile tongue of land on Moloka'i's north side. This had been the infamous site of the leprosy settlement established in 1865 by the *haole* government officials of the king to isolate and separate the largely Hawaiian victims of Hansen's disease, or leprosy. This was only one, albeit perhaps the most horrible, of the plague of diseases that came into Hawai'i after Western contact with Captain James Cook in 1778. Over almost two thousand years, the Native Hawaiian population had grown somewhere between three hundred thousand and eight hundred thousand strong healthy people. There was a fatal flaw in their makeup, however. Isolation had left them with no immunities to even innocuous Western diseases that came in with the whalers and sailors. By 1900, only thirty thousand pure Native Hawaiians were left.

Leprosy was first recorded in the islands in 1840, and it cruelly attacked the Hawaiians with its horrifying disfigurement and eventual death. There was no cure in the nineteenth century, and the Hawaiian government chose this rocky promontory wedged in between the mountains and the sea as a colony for those infected. The location combined isolation with self-sufficiency. A narrow switchback track that tortuously zigzagged down the steep fifteen-hundred-foot sheer cliff was easily guarded. *'Uala*, or sweet potato, and *kalo*, or taro, could be grown on the peninsula. Usually, there were between five hundred and one thousand leprosy victims confined to Kalawao, as the settlement was known. Here Father Damien had achieved martyrdom as he ministered to the forsaken patients. He himself contracted leprosy from his daily contact with and ministrations to the patients. Landings of new patients and supplies were made along the rocky shore, at the rough landing place called Kalaupapa.

There was a terrible beauty to Kalaupapa—the deep furrows on the cliff face, the clouds hiding the summits, and the white surf crashing on the rocks below. In the graveyard of the Kalawao Church, the earth hid the horror of the past and the tragic history of the Hawaiian people. Now a new chapter was added to Kalaupapa's story. A small fleet of Japanese freighters appeared off the point in the middle of 1942 and disgorged a frightened mass of humanity in rafts and lifeboats. Prominent Caucasians were chosen to be the new unwilling refugees of these shores. Eventually their numbers totaled some five thousand souls, from the elite of Hawai'i's society—the descendants of the Boston missionaries. They were the new citizens of "Camp Roosevelt," or as the Japanese called it, "Kanpu Losevelto."

They were dumped ashore with pitifully few supplies or tools. Their hardy New England ancestors had come to these shores in the early nineteenth century with a certitude of belief and self-sufficiency of purpose, stern and dour Calvinists in pursuit of salvation for Hawaiians' souls and land for their offspring. A century of success in both endeavors had provided the Hawaiians the keys to the kingdom, and ensured most of the good land for sugar cultivation for missionary boys. They had become the sugar barons, lording it over the Native Hawaiians and Asian plantation workers in a paternalistic feudalism. Now the tables were turned; they were the frightened and confused immigrants on these foreign shores of Moloka'i, which none of them had ever visited. A century of living easy in big white homes in Nu'uanu Valley, practicing a pious religion at Central Union Church, studying rigorously at Punahou and Yale, and perfecting social graces at the Pacific Club had left them woefully unprepared for this ordeal.

This situation had the makings of a tragic melodrama orchestrated by the Japanese, one of thousands they had perpetrated across Asia and the Pacific since 1931, when they invaded Manchuria, but for one small, simple man. He was William Kamaka, a Protestant minister of Hawaiian descent who remembered the often forgotten good works of the early missionaries—the first schools, a written language, Western medicine, new agricultural products, and a genuine, if sometimes misguided love for the Native Hawaiians. It was these gifts of the missionaries that Reverend Kamaka recognized, that made him accompany the forced migration to be a *kōkua*, or helper. Hundreds of *kōkua*—husbands, wives, sons, and daughters— had come with the leprosy patients to comfort their afflicted loved ones. Now Reverend Kamaka continued this tradition. He was headstrong and brave, ordinary and yet exceptional. He had an appetite to do good, to return the help given by these refugees' ancestors to his people, and a willingness to risk martyrdom.

He knew the old ways, how to plant the land and construct shelters, how to plant hope and courage as well as taro and sweet potatoes. He became the de facto leader of Camp Roosevelt. Word of his deeds spread quickly through the Hawaiian communities on all islands—the Hawaiian Father Damien! The Japanese authorities were engaged in an all-out effort to win the support of Hawaiian people. To remove him or interfere with his work would surely disrupt or even destroy what they had achieved in winning support from the Native Hawaiians. Aware of his growing reputation, William Kamaka cajoled and forced the authorities to provide adequate food and more tools and supplies so the residents of Camp Roosevelt could achieve self-sufficiency and a minimal, yet survivable standard of living. The sons and daughters of the missionaries came through the war and Japanese occupation largely intact. After the war, and Reverend Kamaka's death, they erected a statue of him outside the Central Union Church, and each year they hold a gala dinner to honor both him and the recipient of the Kamaka Award, given to the missionary descendant who has done the most to apply Christ's teachings to the islands. Reverend William Kamaka taught the missionary offspring a lasting lesson in Christian charity and Hawaiian *aloha*.

There were thousands of such stories of hope and heroism in the years of occupation. Despite their losses of land and culture, the Hawaiians never lost their *aloha*, their love for all peoples arriving on the beautiful shores of Hawai'i. This was their great strength, and their great weakness. It left them vulnerable to the diseases passed by close human contact. It left them cheated of their lands by men more greedy than themselves. Now it gave them the strength to endure the final struggles for these islands.

VOICES

15
Togo's Story, Part 2

My second life began in 1920, with the Great Strike of that year. I did not know it then, but the long trek to Honolulu from Kahuku plantation after our eviction marked the end of my boyhood and the transition to a new world. I carried dual citizenship—both Japanese and American. I was born in an American territory, and so I was an American, but by Japanese law, I was also a Japanese citizen. Before 1920, I did not feel this, for I lived mostly in the world of Japan, in the Japanese camp, with parents who spoke only Japanese and celebrated Japanese culture and values. Now I had a chance to enter the American world, for living in Honolulu enabled me to attend McKinley High School—"Tokyo High" it was called, since so many young *nisei* in my situation also went there. McKinley High, with its progressive teachers, was the path to a new world for me. Both from my parents and the plantation mentality, I had learned the values of obedience, duty, place, obligation, and the group. Now I learned of those of equality, opportunity, freedom, individualism, and democracy.

My father had taught me about the traditional Japanese heroes I should emulate: Oda Nobunaga and Tokugawa Ieyasu, the military unifiers of Japan; Saigo Takamori, the upholder of traditional *samurai* values, whom my father's brother had died fighting; and of course Heihachiro Togo, the victor of Tsushima after whom I was nicknamed. Now I learned about George Washington, Thomas Jefferson, Abraham Lincoln, Thomas Edison, and my personal hero, Theodore Roosevelt. Teddy was someone the Japanese people and government especially disliked, because of his role in the settlement of the Russo-Japanese War and his Gentlemen's Agreement to limit Japanese immigration to the United States. He also sent the Great White Fleet around the world to overawe the Japanese. To me, though, he personified the exuberant spirit of America. He also tried to break the power of the American *zaibatsu*—the Trusts—and he tried to preserve the great American wilderness. He was a scholar and writer. He was a brave "rough rider" warrior, an example of the *samurai* spirit and Zen discipline! These men and their ideals often were in conflict with those my father revered, and so I began to find myself and my beliefs suspended between two worlds, Japanese and American. I tried to find a way to hold onto both, to walk a path that blended both world views together, but that was not always possible. I became a "freethinker," so to speak, sometimes Japanese, sometimes American, sometimes conservative, other times liberal, sometimes siding with Democratic and union views, and sometimes with the Republican and business perspective. It was a difficult balancing act, and I wasn't always successful.

My four years at McKinley whetted my appetite for higher education at the University of Hawai'i, but shortly after my graduation in 1925, Father suffered a stroke that left him partially paralyzed, so I had to find work to support us. I had managed the family garden in Kahuku, so now I became a truck farmer on leased land in Waiāhole Valley on the windward side. Being in my own small business gave me an appreciation for what it took to make the land show a profit, and I developed a grudging respect for the planters who made Hawai'i an exporter of sugar and pine. I used to have friendly arguments with Kimo, the old Hawaiian who leased me land. He hated the missionaries and planters who had "stolen" his land and the wealth of the land. I pointed out to him that the original missionaries had done much good here, bringing medicine, education, new agriculture, and of course a new religion. I had admired Francis Xavier, the Jesuit missionary in Japan, and I saw that Hiram Bingham was much the same—strong-minded and dedicated. Most of the missionaries here did not become rich; they died early deaths in poor conditions. Many of their grandchildren became wealthy, but they acquired the land from the Hawaiian *ali'i,* or chiefs, who received 1.5 million acres from the Great Mahele. It was they who sold the land out from under the Hawaiians! Much of the land in central and leeward O'ahu was arid and barren; it had little value until the planters gave it value by bringing water to it through the irrigation ditches and artesian wells. The planters created the wealth that built 'Iolani Palace; they didn't steal it. The biggest land grabber of all, I pointed out, was Kamehameha himself! After conquering O'ahu in 1795 (and sacrificing the O'ahu king at a *heiau*), he took the best lands for himself, now the Bishop Estate. He was also the biggest moneygrubber of them all, even taxing the girls who swam out to the ships to service the sailors. I reminded Kimo that the men in fancy suits who do that to their "girls" on Hotel Street are called "pimps." He did not appreciate my views.

Not that I liked or appreciated the discrimination and the lack of acceptance and opportunity that the Big Five companies practiced. On the plantation, I could see the bottom of this "pyramid" of power the *haole* businessmen had created, their methods of control and coercion. Now I could glimpse the top of the pyramid on Bishop and Merchant streets, where they had their corporate headquarters. They were interlocked through marriage, directorship, membership at the Pacific Club, the Central Union, or "Sugar" Church, and alumni ties from Punahou and Yale. But it had always been so here and elsewhere—interlocking elites. Before, in Japan, it had been the *daimyō* or *samurai* who could cut down peasants with their swords for not bowing fast enough; now it was the *zaibatsu* families and *genrō* politicians who controlled the economic and political system. Before, in Hawai'i, it had been the *ali'i* and *kāhuna* who owned the land and exploited the commoners, as in the sandalwood trade. The chiefs got clothing and jewelry for the valuable sandalwood, and the commoners got pneumonia and malnutrition for their efforts. The chiefs could crush in the skull of a woman who broke the *kapu* by eating a banana or strangle a man who fell into the chief's shadow and defiled his *mana*. Now it was the *haole* planters and businessmen, but in my mind, their time of rule would be short. For there was a document in America called the Declaration of Independence, and it would someday have effect here, just as it had destroyed slavery and the feudalism of the Old South!

VISTAS

16
The Second Great Mahele

I begin this lecture with a quote from General Mori's most important single military directive in Hawai'i:

Imperial General Order 48

I, General Mori, Military Governor of Hawai'i, acting in the name of his Imperial Majesty, order the immediate dissolution of the Anglo-American companies known collectively as the "Big Five": Castle and Cooke, C. Brewer, Theo. Davies, Alexander and Baldwin, and American Factors (seized illegally during World War I from our gallant ally Germany). The offices, buildings, assets, and subsidiary holdings of these companies—the American *zaibatsu*—will become the property of His Imperial Majesty, to be managed by officials of Mitsubishi, Mitsui, Sumitomo, Yasuda, and Nissan, for the collective benefit of the people of Hawai'i and the Greater East Asia Co-Prosperity Sphere.

The reasons for this action are as follows: Anyone familiar with the sad history of Hawai'i in the past century knows that American economic and political interests moved into the kingdom of Hawai'i and gradually wrested away from the native peoples of Hawai'i their economic and political destiny. The principal measure for this theft was the Great Mahele of 1848, which imposed an alien land ownership on the Hawaiian people and began the process of land alienation from Hawaiians to the haoles. This quasilegal manipulation was largely complete by the turn of the century, with most of the good farming lands in the hands of the Big Five. By 1886, two-thirds of the government lands were in the hands of the haoles through sales and leases, and by 1936, only six percent of the *kuleana* lands were still in the hands of the commoners. Their focus was on export crops—sugar and pineapple for corporate profits rather than local food crops and self-sufficiency. This "great *mahele*," instead of restoring the vigor and numbers of Hawaiians, hastened their demise, requiring the planters to import thousands of Asian workers—Chinese, Japanese, and Filipinos—to slave in the cane and pine fields. Thus, the combination of American capital, native land, and Asian labor enriched the children of the missionaries here and delivered Hawai'i into the hands of the annexationists in 1898 while it impoverished the Hawaiians and exploited the Japanese. The *dōhō* built Hawai'i for sixty years with their sweat and labor on the plantations, and the losses and sacrifices of these two peoples, Japanese and Hawaiian, shall be rectified.

As the principal measure for correcting this century-long injustice, the lands owned and leased by the "Big Five" shall be immediately confiscated and made available to persons of Hawaiian and Japanese ancestry through a second Great Mahele—a reverse land distribution and ownership system. Any individual of three-quarters Hawaiian blood ancestry and pure Japanese ancestry is eligible for a land grant of five acres, providing he begins immediate cultivation of crops, livestock, and produce deemed suitable for local consumption. Speed is of the essence, as Hawai'i faces an acute food shortage due to wartime conditions. It is noted that this order is issued March 8, 1942—the ninety-fourth anniversary of the original Great Mahele of March 8, 1848.

So began the social and economic transformation of Hawai'i under the empire of Japan. The announcement of the land confiscation and redistribution had an electrifying effect in the Hawaiian and Japanese communities. Thousands of Hawaiian families had lost their *kuleana* lands generations ago; many had seen their hopes raised, then dashed, with the promise of the Hawaiian Homes Act of 1920. Thousands of Japanese families had given up any hope of ever owning land in the "paradise" of Hawai'i. The haoles controlled over twenty-five million acres of Hawai'i's land—almost fifty times the land owned by Japanese-Americans! Now this was about to change. The response was overwhelming; long lines formed outside the land commission registration centers set up all over the islands. Within a month, fields that had once grown sugarcane and pineapples were cut down, plowed up, and replaced with fields of vegetables and fruits and livestock. Anyone flying over the Hawaiian Islands before and after the economic revolution would have been convinced that these were two different island archipelagoes!

Instead of long lines of plantation gangs planting or cutting cane under the watchful eyes of lunas on horseback, now there were families and friends laughing and singing as they worked their own lands with their own hands. The Native Hawaiians and Japanese Americans supported these far-reaching reforms, and at the same time were achieving a measure of economic self-sufficiency.

Along the beautiful coastlines of windward O'ahu and other islands, the long-neglected fishponds built by Hawaiian ancestors were lovingly repaired and restored, and stocked with fish once again. Deep in the watered green valleys, fields of taro reappeared for the first time in generations, while on the less well watered lands, fields of sweet potatoes, bananas, and oranges flourished once again. Rice fields, with their elaborate irrigation systems, were carved out across the wet, underutilized upslope lands.

Windward O'ahu was the center of much of this activity. Once the center of Hawai'i's first Polynesian settlement almost two thousand years ago, because of its inherent fertility and lushness, windward Oʻahu became a battle prize after Kamehameha the Great conquered Oʻahu in 1795. After a century of neglect and misuse, the land was restored as the "breadbasket" of Oʻahu. The vast Kawainui Marsh, once a great center of taro production, became that once again. Kāneʻohe Bay became the center of a large fishing fleet that ranged hundreds of miles from the coasts, and a thriving fish market rapidly grew up in sleepy Kāneʻohe town. Windward water that had been diverted to leeward Oʻahu sugar was returned to restore the natural stream flows off the *pali*. The revival of the agricultural sector in Hawaiʻi reversed a century of urbanization, and the rural lifestyle rapidly revived.

The rapid economic transformation was not enough to make up for the shortfalls and limited imports from Japan. The Japanese military government imposed heavy rationing to meet the food emergency, and daily calorie intake declined for a majority of the population. The flow of imported foodstuffs from America had ceased, of course, and Japan was twice as far away, with neither the food supplies, transport ships, nor inclination to feed the greatly expanded population. Japanese troops had first priority. Systematic confiscation of food, clothing, and other essentials became common practice across the islands. Hoarding and black market activities led to increasingly harsh punishments; finally, to summary execution. To keep down unrest and potential rebellion against the increasingly harsh measures, opium was at first tolerated, then promoted openly and sold on the streets. Opium dens once again reappeared in the dark recesses of Chinatown. This worked against the various sanitation and inoculation measures undertaken throughout the islands by the Japanese military authorities. Workers in the now Japanese-owned enterprises were brutally exploited by the new economic masters. Strikes and sabotage, and the fledgling labor movement, were crushed mercilessly. Not a few workers ironically longed for the good old days of *haole* planters and lunas on horseback.

Changes were seen throughout the islands. Off the coast of Maui, the mother humpback whale breached the blue waters with her calf close by. For hundreds of generations, these gentle giants had returned to the Hawaiian Islands from their long migrations to give birth. Knowledge of their life patterns had made them easy prey for the whalers a century earlier, and the humpbacks had been driven to the edge of extinction by the hundreds of whaling ships based in Lahaina and other whaling ports. The discovery, in 1859, in the little town of Titusville, Pennsylvania, of petroleum for heating, lighting, and mechanical energy had saved them, and had changed the world in the process. The embargo of American oil to Japan in 1941 had driven the empire to a reckless attack on Pearl Harbor the year before and the subsequent invasion. Now, by an ironic twist of fate, the great humpbacks were again in mortal peril.

Imagine this scene: The spotters on the Japanese whaling ship saw the mother breach, and bore down on her track. The great whale was no match for her mechanical hunter. The steam-driven harpoons pierced her side in a half-dozen places, turning the blue ocean red with blood and froth. The thrashing creature had no way to warn off her calf, and it too fell victim to the whaling ship. Soon both mother and calf were dragged ashore to the processing plant in Lahaina. The greasy black smoke belched out by the plant's high chimney was soon all that was returned to the elements; the blubber, the oil, the bone—all were utilized efficiently and economically by the new money overlords.

Changes loomed on several fronts. Just eight months after the victory of Japanese forces in Hawai'i, a solemn torchlight parade took place in Honolulu. Led by chanters intermixed with those blowing conch shells, Hawaiians in *malo* and tapa carried *koa* wood platforms covered with ti leaves down the streets of the city. On the platforms were the sacred regalia of the monarchs of Hawai'i: the royal feather capes, the crowns of King Kalākaua and Queen Kapi'olani, and the royal thrones. These had been in storage or on display at the Bishop Museum since the overthrow of the monarchy in 1893. Now they were being returned to their rightful place, the newly restored monarchy in the newly restored ʻIolani Palace.

One of General Mori's first major acts had been to proclaim the restoration of the Hawaiian monarchy in April, on the emperor's birthday. Even before that, he had ordered work to begin on the restoration of the royal palace, home of five of Hawaiʻi's kings and queens. Originally constructed in 1882 for King David Kalākaua, the Merrie Monarch, the palace had long been a detested and costly symbol of all the Protestant and republican businessmen of Honolulu hated: royal extravagance, Hawaiian pride, and under Queen Liliʻuokalani, the restoration of native political power, stripped from her brother by the Bayonet Constitution of 1887. When the queen announced her intention to proclaim a new constitution in 1893, the business-men struck, aided by the American minister and U.S. Marines. The queen was deposed and later imprisoned in the palace for her complicity in a counterrevolution.

The despised palace was looted of much of its furnishings through confiscations, sales, and auctions. The palace itself became just another office building for the Provisional Government, later the Republic of Hawaiʻi, and then with annexation by the United States in 1898, for the Territory of Hawaiʻi. King Kalākaua's bedroom suite became the territorial governor's office, and the beautiful throne room and state din-ing room became the seat of the House of Representatives and Senate. Years of neglect, abuse, tropical rot, and termites had left their mark. The gradual destruction of the palace mirrored the physical decline of the native population, and General Mori was determined to reverse both. Despite the shortage of resources and skilled manpower, Mori ordered work on the palace restoration and the recovery of the palace furnishings. The homes of the *haole* elite, in Kāhala and Nuʻuanu Valley, were raided, and suspected palace belongings were confiscated.

Many of the homes themselves were eventually taken over for the comfort of the Japanese *zaibatsu* executives who made their way to Hawai'i. Japanese officials had much practice in China and elsewhere in extracting information about hidden assets—jade, jewelry, silver, and gold.

In the minds of the Japanese leadership, what had happened in Hawai'i was part of Anglo-Saxon takeover of Asia and the Pacific, leading to a destruction of Asian culture, labor exploitation, and land alienation, so that by 1900, virtually all of Asia and the Pacific Islands, except Japan, were part of the European colonial system. Only Japan had escaped this imperialism, first by destroying the Christian missionary movement in Japan, then by closing Japan for more than two hundred years in a self-imposed isolation under the Tokugawa Shogunate. During those two centuries, however, Japan had fallen behind in the military and economic fields—bows and arrows and swords against steamships and big guns. With the overthrow of the shogunate in 1868 and the Meiji Revolution over the next three generations, Japan entered the ranks of the Great Powers, defeating in turn China, Russia, and then the Western powers of Britain, France, Holland, and America in Asia in the opening years of the Great Pacific War. Japan now sought to replace these powers in the leadership of Asia and the Pacific. The Pacific was seen as the "New Sea of Japan"—the Shin Nipponkai, an "Asian Ocean," restored to its "natural unity."

Hawai'i had a special place in the Co-Prosperity Sphere. In addition to the strategic considerations—Hawai'i in American hands as a "dagger in the heart" of Japan—there were the many historical and cultural ties between Japan and Hawai'i. Hawaiians, as Polynesians, were seen as Asians in Japanese anthropological theory. The Japanese victory meant Hawai'i's return to Asia. Historical accounts placed the arrival of the first Japanese in Hawai'i at Makapu'u Point in the thirteenth century. King Kalākaua's call for Japanese leadership to organize a "Federation of Asian Nations" rang down through the years, and there was much regret in Japan for failing to expel the American annexationists in 1893 when the queen was deposed, and for failing to occupy Hawai'i before the 1898 annexation by the United States. Now that failure was finally rectified; Asia and the Pacific had been "cleansed" of Anglo-Saxon "pollution" by the Holy War of 1941–42, and the Pacific finally unified, from the "western anchor" of Singapore to the "eastern anchor" of Hawai'i. As part of this "natural unity," thousands of Japanese and Okinawan farmers and settlers began to arrive in Hawai'i in late 1944 and early 1945 as Japan integrated and strengthened her hold on Asia and the Pacific. The fear (or excuse) of the American annexationists of 1898 was being fulfilled fifty years later by this new wave of Japanese in Hawai'i.

Behind the high ideals and rhetoric, however, the realities of Empire were the same for the Western and Eastern Powers. The Greater East Asia Co-Prosperity Sphere proved to be more brutal and exploitative than the European colonies had been, but the forces of change set in motion by the Japanese conquest would have far-reaching consequences across Asia and the Pacific, including Hawai'i. That, however, was in the future. For now, General Mori had taken momentous steps in restoring the monarchy and restoring the land. He had set changes in place that could not be stopped or reversed. The "life of the land" was being perpetuated in right use-ness.

VOICES

17
Togo's Story, Part 3

Admiral Togo's great naval victory over the Russians at Tsushima Straits had been a source of immeasurable pride for my father and the *issei* of his generation. That was in the year of my birth, 1905, and it earned me my nickname and also gave me an abiding interest in naval affairs and strategy. Now that I was living in Honolulu instead of the cane jungle of Kahuku, I could see the ocean every day. I visited the harbor when warships came to Hawai'i, and I could acquire books about naval history and battles. The year of my birth really marked the beginning of Japan's overseas empire, for victory over Czarist Russia (and China ten years earlier) gave her control over Korea, which she annexed in 1910. The victory over Russia occurred just seven years after the United States had become a Pacific power with the annexation of Hawai'i, Guam, and the Philippines following her victory in the Spanish-American War of 1898. By 1920, the year I moved to Honolulu and began my new, second life, the course was set for future conflict between the two nations of my citizenship. Japan had acquired the islands of Micronesia—the Marshalls, Carolines, and Marianas—from defeated Germany as "mandates," or colonies, under the League of Nations. Now the United States and Japan had "overlapping Pacific empires"!

Although the United States had created a U.S. Pacific Fleet by 1920, we made the concession to Japan at the Washington Naval Conference not to fortify Guam and the Philippine Islands. But this not only created a military vacuum and a tempting target for the empire of Japan; it also left the Japanese embittered by the treaty-based ship reduction and inferiority to America and Britain. Both claimed the need for an Atlantic and a Pacific fleet. Proud Japan was also offended by the American Immigration Law of 1924, the Japanese Exclusion Act, which by implication branded the Japanese as an inferior and undesirable people for emigration to the United States. For a time though, relations between Japan and the United States seemed to settle down into an amicable situation. Japan had a period called the Taisho Democracy, and America experienced the Harding and Coolidge prosperity of the Roaring Twenties.

As a graduation present from McKinley High School in 1925, one of my teachers who knew of my love of naval affairs gave me a copy of the newly published *The Great Pacific War*, by British naval writer and strategist Hector Bywater. I read with stark fascination Bywater's prophecy of all-out naval war between the United States and Japan, beginning with a surprise Japanese attack that would destroy much of the U.S. Pacific Fleet, followed by an invasion of Guam and the Philippines. In Bywater's book, the United States responds with a series of amphibious, island-hopping assaults through the Central Pacific, culminating in the recapture of the Philippines, despite suicide attacks by Japanese ships and planes. The Japanese Fleet, in Bywater's account, is lured from its protective anchorage into a decisive naval battle, and Japan loses the war due to the overwhelming concentration of forces brought by the United States.

Soon the prosperity of the 1920s increased world trade and reduced world tensions, and I put the book aside as a realistic but fanciful account of an unlikely scenario.

My life turned to more personal matters. I had gotten married in the last year of high school and had a daughter, Florence, and a son, Ted, soon thereafter. With a family to support and a farm to run, I put aside my interest in international affairs, and so, it seems, did everyone else in America. The year 1919 in Hawai'i turned out to be the high point of good relations between the Japanese community here and the rest of the islands' peoples. That year, the big event was the dedication of the Phoenix Fountain in Kapi'olani Park, commemorating the fifth year of the new Japanese emperor's coronation. The fountain was paid for by funds from the Hawai'i Japanese community, and thousands turned out for the dedication ceremony, with the Japanese Consul General as the main speaker. After the presentation were the prayers and "banzais."

The next year saw the Great Strike and a wave of anti-Japanese feelings, marked by the attempts to destroy, then "regulate" the Japanese language schools. Then there were the Fukunaga and Massie trials of the late twenties and early thirties, both involving murder, kidnapping, and a double standard of justice that inflamed racial and ethnic tensions in the islands. My wife and I, however, concentrated on raising our son and daughter.

With the 1930s came the Great Depression and hard times for everyone, especially in Japan, a nation heavily dependent on trade for raw materials and markets. Japan began her military expansion into Manchuria in 1931 and China in 1937. My father and his generation were caught up in a patriotic wave, taking up collections and buying Japanese war bonds for the New Order in Asia, with the proclaimed mission to free Asia and the Pacific from the Western colonial powers and create the Greater East Asia Co-Prosperity Sphere. American policy turned increasingly against Japanese military actions in China and elsewhere and her alliance with Nazi Germany. When World War II broke out in 1939, Germany quickly defeated France and Holland, and Japan took advantage of the situation by taking over French Indochina. The United States responded with an oil embargo against Japan in 1941, forcing the Japanese into a no-win situation. Japan had less than two years' oil reserves, so the choice was either a humiliating retreat or a bold strike south, to the oil fields of the Dutch East Indies. As these events unfolded, I dug up my fifteen-year-old copy of Bywater's book and reread his predictions with horror and grief.

I knew what was coming; the two halves of my world were coming apart. When I heard the bombs falling on December 7, I knew in my heart what a terrible future was in store for us!

VISTAS

18
The North Pacific Wall

General Order of the Imperial High Command for Hawai'i

      Officers and Men of the Hawai'i Occupation and Defense Force, you carry a special responsibility in the defense of the empire. We are stationed thirty-five hundred miles from the home islands, on the outer defense perimeter of the Greater East Asia Co-Prosperity Sphere. We have driven the American imperialist forces back some three thousand miles to their own western coast. Forcing the Americans to make such a long retreat marks one of the most glorious victories in the long history of the Japanese military forces! You are to be congratulated. Intercepted radio broadcasts from America and elsewhere make it clear that the United States has, for the time being, accepted our hegemony over the Central and Western Pacific Region. As America is also engaged in war with our European Allies of the Axis Pact—Germany and Italy—their government has announced that their priority will be to aid their allies in Europe—Britain and Russia—who are at this moment on the verge of defeat. As expected, the Americans have abandoned their Asiatic allies, the Chinese and Filipinos, in favor of their white Anglo-Saxon and Slavic brothers. There is no doubt of the final outcome on the European Front; both Britain and Russia will be crushed. America will, at that time or later, turn back to regain her

Hawai'i and Philippine colonies. We must be ready for this; we cannot sit back and be unprepared, as the Americans were at Pearl Harbor on December 7 of last year. Therefore, specific orders are being prepared for the transformation of O'ahu into an island *toride*—fort. In this massive undertaking, prisoner and civilian labor will be freely conscripted to meet our needs. Every man must do his utmost in this undertaking, we the *samurai* of Japan's front line, of the North Pacific Wall!

The main Japanese invasion force had landed along O'ahu's North Shore, a fifteen-mile stretch of beach running from Ka'ena Point to Kahuku Point. This was the "back door" to Pearl Harbor and Honolulu, and it was now to be closed by the construction of a massive set of fortifications near the beaches. American defensive plans had relied on a mobile defense force based at Schofield Barracks in Central O'ahu, high on the "saddle," and able to move into coastal positions, backed up by coastal artillery and mobile rail-mounted guns. Clearly it had not worked.

The construction by the American army of massive concrete bunkers along O'ahu's scenic North Shore would have been seen as an intolerable intrusion by the local population. This was not a problem for the Imperial Japanese Army, however, and so it was done. For the northern and eastern coasts, military planning called for stopping the American invaders on the beaches. This meant massive concrete bunkers, pillboxes, and gun emplacements near the beaches for maximum fire onto the landing areas. Quarries were expanded, and new ones opened, to supply the stone and cement for this string of fortifications. The millions of tons of materials used for this, the most ambitious construction project in Hawai'i's history, were transported on the O.R. and L.—the O'ahu Railway and Land Company railroad. Completed in 1899 by business tycoon Benjamin Dillingham, this 36-inch-gauge rail line ran the length of the North Shore. In peacetime, it had served passengers for outings and picnics far from Honolulu. The 170 miles of track converged at the main O.R. and L. Station in Iwilei on North King Street. Now it served a more sinister purpose. At either end, American prisoners did the loading and unloading.

The main concrete bunkers, every two hundred yards or so, were interspersed with smaller pillboxes, with no blind approaches. Many key positions were connected with tunnels hacked out of the coral bedrock by sweating prisoners and lines of exhausted back-ups passing the buckets and large chunks of coral down to form an unbroken wall, behind which were trenches, rifle pits, and machine gun nests. Other prisoners and Japanese troops strung barbed wire along the front, or placed beach obstacles at the direction of shouting Japanese officers. Prisoners who moved too slowly or collapsed of heat prostration were summarily shot or beaten savagely. If they were still alive at the end of the day, they were thrown into the railway car and hauled to the nearest temporary POW camp. The long trip back to Diamond Head wasted several hours of work time each day, so work camps were created, and the prisoners were rotated, worked mercilessly, then given a brief time to recuperate before the process was repeated.

In addition to the main line of bunkers, caves were hollowed out in the surrounding hillsides to house artillery and antitank guns. Each gun was protected by ten or more mutually supporting machine gun emplacements. In places where the sandy soil did not provide a solid foundation for the massive concrete structures, the Japanese forces built less permanent bunkers reinforced with layers of sand and coconut logs, honeycombed with tunnels and trenches for communications and reinforcements. Along the northeast coast, where the mountains come down close to the sea, high caves were mounted with light artillery hauled up the cliffs with winches and cables. Barracks were built at Kahuku, Lā'ie, Hau'ula, Punalu'u, and Ka'a'awa to house mobile Japanese defense forces along that narrow coast. The scenic bay at Kāne'ohe, with its patches of white coral in the shallow blue-green waters, was ringed with light artillery and mortar batteries. Along the entire northern and eastern coasts of Oʻahu, the Japanese laid thousands of floating and submerged mines. Surfing along the coasts became a very risky business, as several daring but unlucky surfers discovered. When their long, heavy wooden surfboards hit the submerged contact mines, there was a muffled explosion, and a plume of water rose as they were instantly transformed into bloody chum. Wooden splinters of their once beautiful boards and shreds of their two-piece cotton bathing suits drifted ashore to mark the spot where these intrepid challengers of the Banzai Pipeline met the realities of warfare in the twentieth century.

The most concentrated set of defenses, however, was the East Oʻahu Military Zone. Beyond the hills to the south of Kailua, through Waimānalo and around Makapuʻu Point to the Kuliʻouʻou Ridge, the Japanese army sealed off the entire southeastern end of Oʻahu to create a massive fallback defensive position—the Hirohito Line, as it came to be called. The flat plain of Waimānalo, site of the Bellows Air Station, was transformed into the major Japanese military base in the islands. The air station was enlarged into a major airfield capable of handling bombers unloaded off the carriers. Workers constructed rows of wooden barracks interspersed with bomb shelters and weapons storage caches. Beyond Waimānalo, the Makapuʻu cliffs rose steeply over the jagged coastline and crashing surf to form a natural barrier far superior to anything the hand of man could create. The cliffs also were attacked by gangs of sweating men, hollowing out tunnels and gun mounts. The one narrow road, Kamehameha Highway, which snakes up the side of the cliff over Makapuʻu Beach, was set with explosive charges underneath to blow it up, and similar charges in the cliffs above it to turn it into a pile of rubble.

On both approaches to the eastern Koʻolaus, the swamps and marshlands of Kuapā and Kaʻelepulu bordering the East Oʻahu Defense Zone became "mine swamps"—minefields and tank traps preventing armored and mechanized units from proceeding from either direction into the central defensive enclave. On the far eastern end of O'ahu, Koko Crater dominates the skyline. Its rounded dome rises twelve hundred feet into the air. This distinctive, gentle volcanic cone was destined to become the "Mount Suribachi" of the Battle of O'ahu. Here Japanese forces prepared for the final battle, preparing defense in depth with increasing lethality as one approached the crater and its summit.

One side of the crater had eroded through, and this allowed Japanese defense forces to line both the inside and outside walls of the crater with an extensive system of tunnels and caves. The crater was honeycombed inside and outside; the surface structures blended in with the lava rock landscape exterior. The several huge underground chambers held three hundred to four hundred soldiers each. Their multiple entry points and exits, with interconnecting passages, combined mobility with fixed positions. The deep erosion gullies along the entire exterior of Koko Crater made it possible for the military engineers to set up overlapping machine gun posts and sniper nests. It was called the "Meatgrinder" by the American forces who assaulted it three years later. A smaller-scale version of this defensive system was constructed on Koko Head, overlooking the flooded crater called Hanauma Bay. On the rare breaks in the work, prisoners were allowed to swim there and catch fish in the shallow crater lagoon. The beauty of the tropical setting belied the awful conditions under which the American prisoners of the Japanese labored. Along beaches where once the Hawaiians had fished, and more recently *haole* servicemen and their dates had passionately made love, some of these same men were now sweating laborers. The scene was one of misery and pain, never to be forgotten. Altogether, some sixteen miles of tunnels snaked underground in the East O'ahu Military Zone.

Hundreds of lives were sacrificed over the next three years to make "Fortress O'ahu" impregnable, but the worst of the defense labor projects was the trans-Koʻolau railway and its infamous tunnel. From the windward side of Oʻahu, only the Pali Road snaked along the cliffs, up twelve hundred feet from the base and into Nuʻuanu Valley. The windward coast road, Kamehameha Highway, ran seventy miles up the coast to the North Shore and over the "saddle" of the Central Plain to leeward. A handful of American soldiers had held the Nuʻuanu Pass for some days against the Japanese invasion force before they had been overwhelmed from the rear. The Japanese defense planners determined to build a railroad line and tunnel through the Koʻolau Mountains—a defense highway to quickly move troops and supplies across island.

The route they chose was through North Hālawa Valley on the leeward side to Hāʻikū Valley on windward Oʻahu. This required the digging of a five-thousand-foot tunnel through the mountain at a one-hundred-foot elevation in the rear of the valley, and a long trestle track down the side of the sheer cliffs in Hāʻikū Valley. Work crews of prisoners were brought to both sides of the island, and they began the infamous Hālawa-Hāʻikū Railroad, a miniature version of the Burma-Siam Railroad in Asia. Teams of prisoners first cleared the heavy undergrowth of these once heavily populated valleys, and then the main construction teams proceeded to excavate and level the railroad bed. Under the direction of Japanese engineers, logging crews cut and dragged the heavy logs with chains and rollers to the rear of the valley. Here they were squared and cut into suitable timber for the trestle, and slowly it began to rise to meet the valley wall. In the rear, crews laid the railroad ties and then dragged the heavy iron rails up the valley, hammering them in place with iron spikes. The quiet green valleys echoed with clanging metal.

High above them, the prisoner mining crews had begun the tunneling. There was limited use of explosives; picks, shovels, and baskets were the principal tools used—those plus the wasting muscles and energy of hundreds of prisoners. As the tunnel through the soft lava rock progressed, clouds of fine tuff particles filled the air, half blinding the prisoners and filling their lungs with asbestos-like dust. Prisoners were worked to exhaustion, then replaced in the front ranks by new teams. Behind them, rows of prisoners hauled the debris and spoil from the tunnel in woven coconut baskets and dumped it down the side of the cliff. The thin rice gruel soup did not replace or replenish the body tissue used up, and the men of the tunnel work died by the score, only to be replaced by a "fresh" batch of already half-starved men. With the forced pace of work, serious accidents and injuries were daily occurrences, especially cave-ins. Men were crushed or maimed for every few feet of tunnel dug out of the mountain. After nearly one-and-a-half years of brutal labor, the tunnel workers broke through on the windward side. There was no cheering or celebration; too many had suffered and died in the process. Workers in Hā'ikū Valley had also constructed a railroad trestle up the side once a roadbed had been chipped out of the face of the cliff by gangs of ragged men on bamboo scaffolding. Dozens of men had fallen to their deaths in this epic struggle with the mountain also. Their bodies and bones intermingled with those in the much older sites of human sacrifice on the war *heiau* of the Hawaiian kings.

After nearly two years of work and 1,778 deaths related to the railroad, the line was opened with much celebration. The *haku lei* stretched across the track was cut with a *samurai* sword after a blessing by the leading Hawaiian *kahuna*, or priest. The first train through the tunnel overflowed with Japanese officers and selected Hawaiian leaders and local Japanese community leaders. The little Dillingham steam locomotive, brightly festooned with the rising sun (or "meatball" as the Americans called it) flag, chugged up the grade of the trestle with its steam whistle piping. A Japanese military band played patriotic tunes from the little caboose. From a distance, the scene resembled a toy train set in a department store window. In the first car, King Stephen Kamāmalu and General Hiro Mori sat proudly, while the starved and overworked prisoners who did the labor were marched back to the POW camp in Diamond Head Crater. The railroad and tunnel, now the Hawai'i Defense Road, have been remembered with bitterness ever since.

After three years of unremitting forced labor, the coastal defenses of O'ahu were still incomplete. Much of the leeward coast, from 'Ewa to Kāhala, remained unwalled. Instead mines and beach obstacles served as the principle deterrents to the expected landings. The rest of O'ahu, however, was ringed in concrete and steel, or protected by its steep cliffs and crashing surf. In the thirteenth century, *samurai* warriors under the Kamakura Shogunate had walled the beaches of Kyushu against the expected return of the Mongol hordes. Their strenuous and valiant efforts, plus the *kamikaze*, or "divine wind," had saved Japan from the barbarians. Now, seven hundred years later, history, it was hoped, would repeat itself in a far-flung outpost of the empire. Behind Hitler's Atlantic Wall in the west, and Hirohito's North Pacific Wall in the east, the soldiers of the Axis waited for the onslaught of the Allies.

VOICES

19
Flo's Story: A Rough Start

The day I graduated from the University of Hawai'i I became first in my family to hold a college degree. It was in nursing. My father was so proud that he invited all of our friends to our house—something he rarely did because it was so small—and we talked and drank until the early morning. My father thought he was modern, but he had a lot of old attitudes and ideas. He usually didn't like me to drink alcohol, for example. But on that night, in 1940, he bought several magnums of imported *sake* and served drinks free to anyone who would toast my graduation. I remember being slightly embarrassed by the way he made everyone promise the toast before he poured the *sake*. I was grateful, though, and I still am.

On the other hand, I sometimes wish I'd never gotten that nursing degree. With it I experienced more of the war than I ever wanted.

I didn't even have a job lined up when the bombs fell on Pearl Harbor in December. I was thinking of going to the mainland—to get some experience to bring back with me to Hawai'i. I got plenty of experience without leaving Hawai'i at all after December 7, 1941.

We were on the windward side, driving in my father's truck.

He was an early riser, and had work to do, so we'd been awake for nearly three hours already by eight a.m. I was with him because I wanted to do some shopping in town and get in touch with a local hospital, on the off chance they might have a place for me. We'd heard the droning of aircraft engines all morning, but didn't think much of it. The army was always practicing, and bringing in new planes. Their sound was nothing new. It never occurred to me to listen for engines with a different pitch. I just wasn't interested in military things.

We caught the news at eight o'clock, as we finished gassing up the truck at a service station that had a radio. The attendant mentioned that the station had been broadcasting all night—an unusual occurrence, and, as we would later learn, a beacon for the Japanese flyers as much as for the flight of American bombers the army intended it for.

But as I said, at eight we happened to be near a radio, so we heard the announcement that Pearl was under attack as my father was paying for the gas. I remember just sitting there, stunned. I felt nothing. My mind was moving fast, though, so fast that everything around me seemed to be in slow motion. My father's face, eyes wide, slowly swiveled toward first the radio, then me. He forgot his change, and so did the attendant, whose hands, holding the coins, didn't move as he, too, stared at the wireless. Everything inside me said, "It's happened." I suppose we had been expecting something, but the attack itself, when it came, was a shock.

It's funny the things you remember when you're in shock. I remember feeling stunned that the day was continuing. We were not twenty minutes from the bombing going on, and life was totally normal. The sky was warming up, and the wet green of the windward side of the Ko'olau Mountains, like moss on overgrown rocks, was so deep you felt you would sink into it if you touched it. I remember seeing a whale spout, and thinking the grays were back early this year. I distinctly remember not hearing any explosions. I remember because I willed myself to hear them. I strained my ears, and my shoulders. I must have bunched up real good, because next day I felt sore all around my collarbone.

Then I told my father, "I should go to Pearl. I can help."

He didn't even flinch. He just started his old truck, pulled out into the road, and headed for the Pali Highway. No questions asked. I know his heart must've been breaking, and maybe he thought if he were with me he could protect me somehow, though he must also have known that he would never get into the base with me without some medical skills. Especially since we were Japanese. I wondered if they would let me in.

They didn't. There was too much confusion, especially when the tank farm went up, and the main concern on the base was to secure everything. No one was going in or out. I could hear the fire trucks screaming around, but there were any number of people out there, waiting to get in, even some in uniform. No one went in. I guess I can understand. They weren't yet sure if there was an invasion coming, or exactly what direction the attacks were coming from. They wanted to avoid sabotage.

In town, I showed my credentials and got onto a triage team at a local hospital—the same one, in fact, that I had been planning to visit that morning anyway. The hospital staff was overwhelmed, dealing with as many cases as the navy and the army could get to them, along with the increased number of ambulance calls during the attack. It wasn't just members of the military who paid the ultimate price that day. There were awful burn wounds, a few gunshots—mostly from friendly fire. Anyone who took a round from the Japanese planes rarely lived long enough to get medical care at all.

The raid was completely unexpected. That explains why the scene was sheer panic: sailors running around trying to get to their ships, many of which had been sunk by the time they got to the base; airplanes destroyed on the ground in the tight groupings General Short had ordered to prevent sabotage. When they tried to take off, these pilots were literally bombed out of their cockpits. I didn't see any of them come through triage either.

It wasn't until after things had calmed down that the accusations began. I was asked by a doctor to help out at the hospital full time. I was green, and was not employed by either the hospital or the military, but they needed nurses, and so I came on board. It was a natural continuation of what I had been doing. I was asked not to come back after my third shift. The men, I was told, were distressed by my Japanese appearance. They were afraid I would kill them while they were helpless in their beds. Morale, they said, could be damaged.

Leaving, I felt ambivalent. I could understand their fear, and yet I was angered by it, too. I was as American as the New York Yankees, I thought. But I was also Japanese, I realized, and that came with a shock. I couldn't believe the Japanese had attacked us. I couldn't believe I was Japanese, even as I was calling the Japanese "the enemy" in my conversations with people. For the first time in my life, I felt as if I had to choose an identity. But I couldn't choose, because I was both Japanese and American. Those around me would identify me either by the way I looked or by the way I behaved; most, initially, by the way I looked. I had to accept that, even though it made me unhappy. I tried personally to go beyond it. In my own life, I decided that day, I would support the United States, but I would be who I was, with the lessons, and the languages, my parents had given me. I would have to recognize that some would not understand. But I could also try to change their minds.

So I suppose that was what was on my mind when the war started. Just like everyone else, after December 7 I did not expect the Japanese to mount an invasion. We were probably all too secure in the thought that the United States would never let Hawai'i go. We were certainly not aware of how difficult the strategic and supply situations were. So when the invasion came, and the United States lost the islands, we were in shock once again.

At that point, we Japanese had once again to make the choice of loyalty. My own grandfather, who had always dreamed of going home someday, and had retained his status as a Japanese subject and only a U.S. resident, immediately declared his pleasure that he was now once again living under the rule of the emperor of Japan. He was clearly looking forward to the Japanese occupation.

My father was a bit more ambivalent, having lived his whole life here on O'ahu, but his mind was changed when the land was redistributed and he got a chunk of it. Not only that, he felt that his owning land was an "I told you so" to the old Big Five. His land was carved from their estates, so he had, he thought, been able to get back some of the work his father had put into the plantations. He was pleased with that, and so, though he didn't support Japan in general, he certainly supported General Mori and the occupation in Hawai'i.

My brother and I felt differently. Ted was two years younger and still a student at the University of Hawai'i, where I had graduated. We had lived through a time when my father did relatively well for himself, and when the labor leaders of Hawai'i secured some civilized treatment of nonwhite laborers here. In short, this society offered us everything the United States possibly could. We were at home here, not Japanese living among Americans, but Americans ourselves, part of the diverse population of Hawai'i. We could vote, and we'd been to college.

We'd known other Hawai'i Japanese who'd gotten their education in Japan—*kibei* they were called. They didn't have any advantage over us educationally, and in fact, seemed more confused about who they were when they came back than they had been before they went. It seems they were never fully accepted as Japanese when they were in Japan. There they were treated as inferior. They even had to live in dormitories separate from those who had grown up in Japan, regardless of how well they spoke and read the language. They tended to come back with a chip on their shoulder, defending one viewpoint or another. Some were more nationalistic and in favor of the emperor than most Japanese in Japan. Others were determined to show their loyalty to the United States by ostentatiously parading their patriotism at every opportunity.

By far the worst thing Ted and I saw, though, was families grieving over their *kibei* sons who had been drafted into the Japanese army or navy. Since all Japanese in Hawai'i had dual citizenship, those who did not register their status as "overseas" every year were subject to the Japanese conscription system when they returned to Japan. Many young men who were studying there, regardless of their personal politics, were drafted without ever having a chance to come home. Some did come home—in the invasion of February 1942.

VIGNETTES

20

The View from the Ground

He was called a "coast watcher." He didn't really watch the coast, though. Maybe they still did that in New Guinea. Here, right in the middle of the enemy, he watched everything—beaches, harbor, channels, the sky—and reported it all back through his little portable radio set.

Right now he was watching what had become a common sight in the Hawaiian Islands—common again after nearly a century of gradual disappearance: a Hawaiian outrigger-style canoe, carrying six people, was just beginning to stow its sail after covering the channel from Maui.

They always came in paddling: a lower height profile made them less likely to be caught.

He knew what they were carrying: produce—papayas, vegetables, taro—to be sold on the black market whose existence the Japanese stubbornly refused to admit. There just wasn't enough on O'ahu. So Maui supplied the need. The Japanese garrison there was small, and demand for food was hardly larger than before the invasion on the Valley Isle.

As the sail came down, the coast watcher saw it was already too late. A Japanese motor patrol boat was stealthily approaching the outrigger. It had come within two hundred meters before the crew spotted it. The "pop pop" of small-arms fire echoed over the water and was answered by the unmistakable sound of the Japanese 45-caliber mounted machine gun.

On the canoe, men dropped. Two fell into the water. The other four went into the boat looking for some cover. But the 45-caliber was not merciful. Its bullets raked the side of the canoe, causing little fountains of water along its hull.

He had a good position on top of the Koʻolau Range, in sight of Honolulu on one side and the windward area known as Waimānalo on the other. From here the coast watcher could see the three remaining men trying to crawl over the sides of the small craft and get out before they got hit. Two succeeded, one failed, and the waves between the two boats lifted three limp forms. Sharks would be there soon, thought the coast watcher. He grimaced and wished he could see something that would help defeat these occupiers.

As the canoe sank, the Japanese patrol craft continued to move closer, and now the 45-caliber trained its sights on the two men still moving in the water. The coast watcher had seen this before, too. It was a lesson to those who would be smugglers. If you are caught, you will die. And your body will be left for the sharks and other ocean scavengers. Both men held up their hands in surrender. The first was executed, blood and bullets roiling the water around him.

As the patrol boat finished its business, the coast watcher could not pull his eyes away, sick as it made him. The last survivor, treading water with his legs as he held his hands high, had his head blasted off by the machine gun at point-blank range.

The coast watcher felt a tight knot in the pit of his stomach, and the desire to retch and pound his fist into something at the same time. For a moment, anger blurred his vision.

Wahiawā

The Chinese-American man placed his belt knife back in its

scabbard, tied to his waist beneath the waistband of his worn cotton pants. He stood, straightened, and scuffed dirt over the last mine he'd buried in the road here near Wahiawā, where the largest American encampment had been. Now it was virtually a ghost town—but the Japanese convoys to the North Shore had to come through here, and he was going to take out his share of them. Even if it was the last thing he did. One of these days, he thought, it probably would be.

They were simple, homemade mines, with simple pressure detonators; as soon as there was any weight whatsoever on the top of the case, it exploded. Not sophisticated. Not safe. But this was war, and noncollaborating locals knew to stay away from the roads where these mines were placed. They also knew that they could be pressed into service and forced to drive this road. The irony was that helping the success of the resistance and preserving more lives than one depended on their willingness to sacrifice themselves and drive right over the top, as if they didn't know the mines were there. That was the way this worked.

But the convoys from the North Shore rarely had locals with them. These were sensitive places, where the Japanese expected the Americans to come ashore if they came back, and so the placement and supply of their units there was constantly changing, and a carefully guarded secret—although not as hard to penetrate as the Japanese thought. So these mines would get the right targets. The man shouldered his empty canvas rucksack and walked away toward the Koʻolau Range.

Two days later, the mines did get their targets. A small group of five trucks with a captured American Jeep in the lead rolled over the very patch of road where the man had been standing. The results were immediate when the third truck in line hit the first mine. A brief "whoosh" turned the truck into a shell before any sound could alert the trucks ahead and behind. After the boom, the canvas bed cover ignited, and the few soldiers who had survived the bomb itself began to scream as the intense heat melted boot soles and melded flesh to steel.

The Jeep was next. It lurched up, axles snapped, and landed on its side, rupturing the fuel tank on its underside with no resistance and sparing the lives of the driver and his officer passenger. The rear-seat machine-gunner, unable to leap free, had his right leg caught beneath the side of the Jeep, and was liberated of his life in a slow roast of intense heat. He lost consciousness soon after patches of his skull were exposed through seared, taut skin.

Of the other three trucks, two negotiated the minefield successfully by driving off the shoulder of the road and around the affected trucks. The last truck in line reacted too late, however, and suffered major engine damage as another mine exploded upward through the engine compartment and driver's seat. The driver and his passenger were obliterated in a hail of steel and fire, but the other riders escaped. Their walk back to the main Waikīkī-area camp was long and traumatic, as they alternately experienced shell-shock, survivor syndrome, and exhaustion. All the while, they kept to the side of the road and picked their way home as if in a minefield, fear taking a huge toll on their body strength. When they did get back to camp, they had to be given rest and water for two days; they had been so worried about mines, not one had remembered to drink water during the entire walk back.

Imperial Japanese Headquarters, Honolulu

Reading the reports of these events, Mori frowned. He was angry. Though he had expected this kind of problem, he still didn't like it, and it seemed to be coming from both sides. He couldn't control the brutality of his troops, and his junior officers did not understand that the depth of their brutality only served to heighten the heroic impulses of the resisters—and win more converts to the antioccupation cause. If only he could have more Imperial Way faction officers. They at least understood the gravity of the war and were not simply paper-pushers who didn't understand that on the ground, on the front lines, people had to be treated as people, not ignored or thought of as statistics. Mori was not afraid to use brutality, but it had to serve the divine purpose and further the goals of the empire of Japan and its divine ruler. These fools did not get it. They could not control themselves, and they were drunk on power. He was disgusted.

To boot, the local saboteurs were getting bolder and better. Aside from the convoy incident, Mori listed in his mind other recent events: A Japanese officer had been shot in broad daylight at Aloha Tower pier. The shooter still had not been found on this little rock of an island. Guards near Honolulu Harbor had recently scared off saboteurs just before they exploded several major fuel tanks. The paraphernalia and explosives had been found. The perpetrators had gotten away. They were still at large, too. Thefts of food and medicine from Japanese naval and army stores were on the increase, and the latest attempt had shown that the thieves had no problem risking their lives: these particular culprits, knowing they were cornered, had rushed the guards in a charge that reminded Mori of Japanese army final tactics—no quarter given, no attempt to survive made. Just take as many with you as you can.

His hard work would pay off only if he could find a way to make the islanders accept Japan. He could see it clearly. The sabotage and the brutality needed to be stopped, or these islands would be useless to Japan. The more sabotage, the more maintenance cost, and Mori knew that the Imperial High Command was not willing to pour money into an open pit. The more brutality, the more sabotage, he also knew.

His thoughts turned to Imperial High Command. They saw the Hawaiian Islands primarily as a convenient outpost. They were to be self-supporting, ready to face the United States at any time, a first line of defense or a bargaining chip. Strategically speaking, Hawai'i was only a convenient way to push the U.S. Navy far enough away from Japan to make it impotent. Therefore, the cost of maintaining Hawai'i was expected to be very low. So low, in fact, that any disturbance here could bring the army down hard; mass starvation of the local population would be acceptable to certain elements in the Control Faction of the army, if that was what it took to keep the islands secure.

Mori had worked hard at a compromise. He wanted to see the Hawaiian Islands brought into the empire at a minimal cost, but not through violence or starvation, which would only lead to greater cost later, when the whole population supported the resistance. He wanted to get the islanders to cooperate in their own captivity, to agree to be a part of the Greater East Asia Co-Prosperity. If they wanted to be with Japan, they would rout out the resistance themselves, and no one could blame Japan for what happened. To see it heading in the current direction worried him. His legacy, and his status in the army, would suffer. He'd also given his word to many in Hawai'i, his private promise to all, that suffering here would be kept to a minimum. Yet neither side would comply with his wishes. Something had to be done, but he could not decide exactly what.

VOICES

21
Flo's Story: Rhapsody in Red and White

I started working with the POWs at Diamond Head only five days after the Japanese victory on Oʻahu. I had no idea at the time that my brother Ted would be one of the men I would treat, or that I would end up moonlighting in an underground clinic for the "comfort women" the Japanese impressed into service to take care of the baser needs of their men. I ended up having to decide on a daily basis how to allocate the supplies I bullied out of the occupiers—how much to use for the prisoners and how much to smuggle out for the women. Needless to say, there was never enough for both.

There is no way to say which of my two jobs was worse. Diamond Head prisoners showed most clearly the mistreatment they suffered. The women suffered just as horribly, though, despite the fact that they were outside the camp. Their injuries were more often internal, in every sense of the word, and therefore harder to treat. Neither group was ever cured of their suffering. They all carried the scars to the ends of their lives.

My first day at the Diamond Head Prisoner of War Camp I was horrified, terrified, sick, and angry. The hardest thing I have ever learned to do I began learning on that day. That lesson was how to take anything in stride—at least outwardly. This is my understanding of what my ancestors in Japan have always called *tatemae*. That is, you show on the outside what is appropriate to show given the circumstances, the people present, and what they expect of you and you of yourself. My time in the camps taught me more than once that outbursts of anger, American style, only invite ridicule from Japanese and get nothing done. On the other hand, proper behavior in the right situations, whether it is "true to your beliefs" or not, gets things done, even among people who despise you, or whom you despise.

The prison guards were people I learned to despise, but to control. I still have a hard time believing that in Japan, as civilians, they would have been as brutal or bloodthirsty. I've always wondered what changed them. It made me think of Joseph Conrad's *Heart of Darkness*, which I read in college. In another life, I might have married one of these men. My father always wanted me to marry someone from Japan. Even as the thought made my skin crawl, I could often visualize these boys in a different setting, working in the fields as my father had done, carrying an ill child to the doctor. What causes inhumanity is still beyond me. I detest it. Yet I cannot fully detest any of those I have met who are guilty of it. It leaves a dirty feeling in my soul. I feel smeared by their inhumanity, and I am often afraid others can see that I have sympathy for those who have tortured and killed. But I can't help feeling that, if you washed them out inside somehow, just as you would a cup of mud, and put them in normal circumstances, you'd have someone completely different.

I learned to control the Japanese guards on the first day at Diamond Head, when I began to learn to control myself—at least on the outside. When I first arrived, they checked everything I carried with me—rifling my handbag, taking off my jacket and hand-searching every pocket. They probably were planning to strip search me, just for fun, as they had another nurse I met who no longer went to the camp. I surprised them. They smiled at each other as I walked in, and said in Japanese that it would be a pleasure to be sure that I had no contraband "about my body." Clearly they saw me as a Japanese-American who never learned to speak her parents' language. When I replied to them in Japanese, and hinted that I knew General Mori and had regular meetings with him about the state of the prisoners, the grins disappeared, and they got down to business, doing their work far more efficiently than they needed to, as the ripped seams in my jacket could attest. I said nothing more. I couldn't. My nerves were completely frayed after that first attempt at bravery, and after that, it was nearly all I could do to keep the tears from welling up in my eyes, out of relief, and out of fear that they might call my bluff.

I nearly cried for a second time when they showed me into the tent that served as an infirmary. It was at the far end of a row of tents in the middle of the camp—what I soon learned the prisoners called the Frying Pan. In the daytime, the bowl of Diamond Head reached 120 degrees. The prisoners were dressed in old, dirty lavalavas, and many had not even those by the end of the second year of confinement. They were sunburned on a daily basis. They had only a couple of cups of water each day. For the first year, the water came from a duck pond, so clearly polluted there was no question as to the cause of the dysentery I treated every day.

The Japanese allowed only a single basin of water in the infirmary for bathing wounds, and a separate pitcher for me to drink. The water was walked to the tent under guard, usually carried by the weakest prisoner they could find. If he even bowed his head to sniff the water he carried, his head would be forcibly held away from it, and he would be severely beaten after delivering it—usually within about fifty meters of the infirmary tent. Needless to say, I usually went about very thirsty, finding as many subterfuges as I could under which to slip a small drink to each of my patients every day. I drank quarts of water every night to relieve my own dehydration.

Bandages were in short supply, and I was eventually forced to tear up my own bedsheets and bring the strips in for bandages. Up to half of those were taken from me by the Japanese guards, needed, they said, for the Japanese who were actually risking their lives and maintaining their honor in this war. I eventually recruited friends and neighbors to rip up their linen, and even to make coarse bandages out of whatever materials we could find. Antibiotics were unavailable, and painkillers were almost impossible to find.

I worked day after day with men who were starving to death before my very eyes. Their sunburns caused severe fevers, sleeplessness, and susceptibility to gangrene, pneumonia, and various skin diseases. Their severe sleep deprivation, starvation diets, and heavy beatings made them more likely to die before the three years of captivity was over than to survive. So many times I almost gave up. I would wake up in the morning feeling I just couldn't get out of bed to face those men again. Every time I treated one problem, another became the chief threat to life in every patient. Those who did make it through are still my personal heroes. What they endured, I can only guess. Yet it was their words of encouragement, and their short "Thanks, doc," that kept me going. I still feel ashamed that I needed the encouragement of the suffering in order to make it through, but I did. I respect them more than I can say.

But the men in the camp were only the most obvious victims. At night, while I drank my quarts of water, I regularly appeared at a clandestine clinic that served the needs of women who had been impressed into the sex trade to service the Japanese. These women included those of Chinese and Filipino origins, with a few Hawaiians as well, but the Japanese seemed to take the most delight in impressing *haole* women into service. It was these white women who were most popular in the "comfort centers" and often endured the greatest extremes of male behavior, from kindness almost amounting to courtship to extreme brutality. All of these women were horribly treated.

Most were young women, taken forcibly from their homes, whose stolen honor could never be salvaged in the eyes of their parents. These girls served every need the soldiers felt, and paid for it in awful ways.

Obviously, the number of abortions was high. I had always abhorred the idea of abortion, but the pleas these girls made as they came in convinced the doctors to make exception after exception. I convinced two women to carry their children to term. One was forced to have sexual intercourse with men right up to the day her child was born, and had to begin again the day after. She was barely able to move, and had to perform even as she could hear her child crying for feeding in the corner of the room. The other lost her baby when two soldiers beat her with broken chair legs until she collapsed, then raped her while she was unconscious. After that, I never argued about abortion again.

Many women came in asking for tubal ligations, to prevent the possibility of ever becoming pregnant at all. Others had sexually transmitted diseases in various stages of advancement. They were supposed to be treated by Japanese doctors, but the treatment often consisted of simple dismissal, or prescription of exercise and a starvation diet, since medicine, especially antibiotics, was in short supply and reserved for the troops.

For these women, I kept back about one third of the bandages I had made. I felt as if I were cheating the men. But they were not the only ones who had a right to survive. I also stole some painkillers and iodine from the infirmary at the Diamond Head camp. The women needed it, and I could get it. I hoped every day that what I took would not be needed to save the life of a prisoner. But I took it anyway, realizing that it might be the one necessary item, because it might also be the one thing that could save a life at the underground clinic for women.

No one bothered me in either clinic about my Japanese ancestry. But I was bothered by the cruelty of the soldiers of

Japan. I could hardly believe that these people came from the same culture as my grandfather—as me. I still have a hard time making that connection. Since the end of the war, I have never seen in the Japanese the kind of cruelty and indifference to human suffering that I saw during those three years, from 1942 to 1945. I still ask myself why and how a person can be moved to commit such acts, and I still have no answers. I pray that future generations will not have to face or commit such cruelty, yet I know that they will, and I fear for them.

VIGNETTES

22

The Problem of Sabotage

August, 1943. Imperial Liaison Headquarters, Royal Hawaiian Hotel, Waikīkī

Mori crushed the paper in his hand. Trucks turned over all the time, he thought, but not due to plywood land mines. This was clearly another incident of sabotage. The saboteurs weren't even trying to disguise this as an accident. They had become much more daring the firmer the Japanese hold on the Co-Prosperity Sphere had become.

His spies weren't getting much information as to who they were. With so few clues, he was beginning to think there was only one way to solve this problem. He was, after all, going to have to use brutal methods of suppression. He just had to find a way to make the brutality look like locals against locals.

Over the last three months, acts of sabotage had multiplied in every part of the islands. Japanese soldiers and sailors, on passes to enjoy themselves, ended up dead, apparently of alcohol poisoning. Two weeks ago one of his supply vessels, as valuable as gold since Japan had only a limited amount of non-military tonnage, had received superstructure damage. An anti-tank bazooka, of all things, had been fired into it from within a crowd on Aloha Tower pier. That had been bold, and the saboteur had gotten away. His watch officers were rebuked and were still ashamed by the incident.

Soldiers were watching their backs and doors in the "comfort houses" on Hotel Street. Beatings of local residents were getting more and more frequent, as soldiers and sailors thought they saw threats in every sneer—and Mori had no choice but to uphold the Japanese side in these incidents no matter what the circumstances, to maintain a clear sense of who was in charge.

So, he asked himself again, who was doing these things? He felt sure it could not be the local Japanese. They were ambivalent toward, but also to some extent proud of the Imperial Forces. Those who had hoped Japan would liberate Hawai'i from its American occupation prior to 1942 were pitifully obvious. No, the Japanese were cooperating.

It couldn't be the Hawaiians. They loved Mori for restoring the king. Mori was sure they didn't honestly believe the Japanese would leave voluntarily and allow them to rebuild their kingdom in a way of their own choosing. But he also thought they would play Japan for all it was worth before they attempted some sort of independence move. Mori smiled at that, not entirely cynically. He knew that for the next several years, at least, the Japanese forces could not leave. There was nothing in these islands Japan really wanted. In fact, possessing them was costing the Imperial Treasury more than it could really afford.

The islands, as far as the Japanese were concerned, were an outpost and a bargaining chip, no more. As long as Japan held them, the military would have to stay, to guard the eastern edge of the empire. If Japan and the United States ever returned to the negotiating table, the military would have to be here to hand back the islands to the United States as a part of a peace deal that recognized most of the other, economically valuable, territories taken in the move "south." Still, he did allow the current puppet administration some leeway in governing locals, administering local law to some extent, and conducting foreign relations with Japan and other territories in the empire.

The newly restored king was in Tokyo, receiving all the appropriate honors and respect due a head of state in Asia. He was meeting as an equal, if not with His Majesty the Showa emperor of Japan, then at least with other symbolic figures such as Pu Yi of Manchukuo, and Sukarno of the former Dutch East Indies. The Hawaiians rightly saw this as a recognition of their sovereign status. If that sovereignty was an illusion, at least he had given them a dream by giving them back their king.

Mori knew the Hawaiians were under no illusions that the Japanese were protecting them. They were well aware of the occupied status of their kingdom, both because they were politically astute, if not experienced, and because it was clear that the Japanese army got the best of everything that was available on the island.

Nevertheless, Mori thought, if the Americans thought they could take back the territory and once again reduce the king to an insignificant citizen, the question of Hawaiian sovereignty would become more important, and violent, than ever. He hoped the violence would peak after the United States received the islands, and not before, during Japan's occupation.

The islanders were not violent now. Mori had done everything he could to be sure of that. He knew if he ever demonstrated publicly to the Hawaiians how little control they really had, it would spark that violence, and the islands would become a hindrance to Japan's efforts. Such a cost might force abandonment.

For now, this was Japanese territory, and he would have to consider the Hawaiians as possible suspects in the saboteur group. In fact, some might be. But as a group, the Hawaiians were busy getting the king's palace and protocol back in order.

So, he thought, neither the Japanese nor the Hawaiians were politically suitable for the kind of punishment Mori expected he would have to use. He could do more damage than good by alienating his two largest support groups through punishment. That left the other two large groups left in the islands: Chinese and Filipinos. (He didn't put it past the small group of whites still free on the island, but their numbers were not large enough, and their race not popular enough, to make a good object lesson.) But contemplating general retribution against either the Chinese or the Filipinos was against Mori's principles. It wasn't that he liked or felt pity for them any more than for the haoles. He was as sure as any Japanese officer that he was a member of the master race of Asia. He just realized that the best cooperation came from people who felt they had a reason to cooperate. To alienate either of these groups through violence would cause trouble further down the line.

23

Ted's Story: Becoming a POW

March 2, 1942

Dear Flo,

I don't know when you'll get this. I plan to hide it under the floor of my room, in that hollow area we made together when we were in high school to hide our cigarettes from Dad. Guess this is a better use for it. I hope that someday you dig this letter out, so you can understand. I don't know if I'll live through what I'm about to do.

I have decided to join the resistance against the Japanese. I know that Grandfather would be disappointed if he knew, and probably would disown me. Please don't tell him. Father might not be too happy, either. I just don't think the Japanese army should be here. It is not that I don't care for Japan. After all, like you, I am Japanese. But this land doesn't belong to them any more than it ever belonged to the United States. The worst thing, I think, is that they can't win.

I don't know what they plan to do with Hawai'i, or why they want it. You know as well as I do how many times they've sent the battleship *Naniwa* here. Every time, we see some officer or other come out to "talk with the subjects of his majesty."

They always say they want to be sure we're all right, and being treated well. But what did they do when Grandfather was working in the cane fields, paying more to the company store than he earned every month, getting further in debt for the right to work his hands to the bone and have a meager meal at night?

What did they do when the Japanese went on strike against the Big Five, and nearly lost the ability to find jobs on the island at all? Nothing. They just lodged a protest with the American government.

So what do they want with this land now? I don't think they have in mind some benevolent return of the kingdom to the Hawaiian people, or to the residents of the islands. I think they're here for some other reason, and that we are just being used in a bigger military game.

So I've decided to join the resistance, and tomorrow is my first lesson in laying mines.

Ted

March 25, 1942

Dear Florence,

Its been a month now since I started this resistance work. It's getting harder to pretend to Father and to you that I am going off to work in the morning every day. I never seem to be able to bring home money to prove it. I may have to move out soon.

I may as well admit that part of the reason I am doing this is that when the United States comes back—and I am sure they will—I want to show that our family worked on the "right" side of things. I think this is a matter of survival for all of us, and with a member in the resistance, perhaps we will be considered loyal. In any case, whatever risk I take seems justified because of that. I hate to be cynical, but I really think it is the only way to be sure we can get along after the Americans take Hawai‘i back.

The other guys I work with think the same. There are some other Japanese in the group. Most, though, are Filipinos and Chinese. We all get along well. They've come to rely on me because I can speak and read Japanese. I've gotten us in to some pretty amazing places, though I never pretend to be army. It turns out I have an accent I never knew about. They would likely look harder at me if I tried to pass myself off as a soldier. Their security is good, and we have to be inventive and take some serious risks doing what we do.

What do we do? We mostly lay homemade mines along Japanese transport routes, then hide nearby and wait for the explosions to begin. We watch because we want to keep a tally of the damage, so we can report it to the Americans when they arrive. Also, we all feel we ought to know what our work does. It is pretty gruesome sometimes. I lie awake at nights with the memories fresh in my head. I will never forget the awful things I've seen and the terrible deaths I have caused. I watch because I feel I owe it to the people I have killed and injured. I need to know their suffering and keep it in my mind all my life, so I never get complacent about what it is I am doing. I make every attack as quick and painless as possible, with minimum damage to people and maximum damage to equipment. Our real goal is to make it too expensive for the Japanese army to stay here.

We think they might be on to us, though. I don't know if there are informers somewhere, or what, but they seem to be getting closer every time we carry out a new attack. We'll have to be more careful.

April 15, 1942

Dear Flo,

Well, by now you've noticed I haven't been home for a couple of weeks. I live somewhere else now. If you look in the old cigarette hole, you'll know why.

I am a resident of the Frying Pan now, and may be seeing you shortly.

They caught me laying mines along an access road on the North Shore. They almost shot me on the spot, but the officer in charge of the patrol was a cool-headed guy, and he had me brought here. I have to say, I almost wish I'd been shot.

The torture has been pretty tough. I don't want you to worry, and I didn't give away anything they didn't already know. My buddies and I had all agreed beforehand that we would give away each other's names, but nothing more. We don't know where most of our supplies and instructions came from, anyway. The whole resistance is run by a cut-out system, so that if we get caught, we can't really give them anything.

Can't say they didn't try, though. I have never been beaten so hard, or imagined the kinds of things they can do to you when they are in the mood to torture. I've had fingernails pulled out and my leg broken by slow, constant pressure. I will tell you that at those times, I wished I knew more about the resistance—I would've given anything to make the pain stop. I'm glad I didn't know, though, because in my more conscious moments I realized the torture probably wouldn't have stopped anyway.

I'm sure you'll someday see the scars I have. I'll spare you with the details, except to say I am all right. I will probably see you sometime soon, and I'm glad, at least, to know I can. Most guys here don't ever get the chance to see anyone they know from outside. I'll find an excuse to be sick one of these days, soon.

Ted

VIGNETTES

24
Missionary Work

October 2, 1943

The view was stunning from the top of Haleakalā in the dawn light. Mori shivered and pulled his cloak around himself more tightly. It was one article of clothing that regulations demanded he have, and for which he had had absolutely no use since February of the year before. Now he was glad he'd followed the regs.

The sun came up over the rim of the vast, sleeping crater—the massive builder of Maui, second largest island in the Hawaiian chain, birthplace, through fire and flying rock, of land in the midst of the waters. The stirring of the waters that had brought Japan up from the depths before time began had been at work here as well—though not so long ago. This, Mori thought, was the perfect place. What better symbol of the brotherhood of Japan and Hawai'i than the place that most clearly reflected the story of the sun goddess Amaterasu in the ancient history of the *Kojiki*. Here, every morning the sun rose above the crater as the goddess must have from her cave, bringing light, and the Japanese imperial family, to the world.

The rocky, desert landscape within the crater began to show

itself. Shadows receded as the sun climbed the rim and peeked inside. Amaterasu, the sun goddess, convinced of her beauty by a look in the mirror, emerging from her cave once again to give the world another day. Tamer of Susano-o the storm god, bringer of order and light, provider of the purifying waters and the rice that nourishes, Amaterasu recognized this place as she recognized all places in her world. She was here now to witness its dedication to her, through a shrine to her son, the Emperor Showa of Japan, direct descendant of Jimmu, first emperor, to whom she had given the sacred regalia and the honor to rule Japan two thousand years before. Her light, Mori thought, would soon see the establishment of the order of the Japanese Empire and the destruction of the unenlightened followers of the storm god worldwide.

As if in answer to his thoughts, the Japanese Shinto priests standing next to Hawaiian *kāhuna* began to shake their paper tassels. The sun caught the towering posts of the new *torī*, marker of Shinto holy places, and sent their shadows racing across the desolate caldera, encompassing even the *heiau*, as if they were meant to exist together. Poetic, thought Mori. Perfect. Here, two peoples became one. Here, the Japanese and the Hawaiians could find some way to live as brother civilizations. It did not matter that the Japanese had the power. The symbolism here was neutral, neither belief system taking precedence over the other. As it should be.

The Hawaiians were now in the midst of an *oli*, or chant, and several strong-looking young men were draping a huge *lei* of island flowers over the *torī* in what made a stunning display in the morning light. If there truly were gods, they must be pleased by this, Mori thought.

When it came his turn to speak, he paused for a moment, carefully turning to look behind him at the rising sun for effect. There were only fifteen people here, but they were all spiritual leaders who would pay attention to what he had to say. Strange as it seemed, he was a bit awed by the presence of Stephen

Kamāmalu, king of Hawai'i. In front of these people, he had now to put Japanese presence in these islands into historical and ideological terms that provided an acceptable reason for the Japanese to be here. They were not pushovers. He was prepared.

"Your Majesty, gentlemen," he intoned. "I will keep my remarks brief. I am not, as you know, qualified to lead people in a religious sense. However, since I do lead people into battle, I have spent some time thinking about death, and its meaning for those of us who live. I am therefore honored to be here at this meeting of two great traditions of understanding the eternal, and I stand in awe of this beautiful place and its dedication to the gods that Japan and Hawai'i, truly, I believe, must share. I wish to proclaim, here, in the sight of Amaterasu, here on Haleakalā, that Japan and Hawai'i are, indeed, brother civilizations. We will support each other until the end of time."

A brief silence greeted his introduction, but he could see all eyes intent upon him. No one looked at the sky or the ground. He had made contact.

"It is, therefore, with a great sense of purpose that I make the following announcements upon this solemn occasion. As you know, during your great king's recent tour of Japan, he met regularly with his Majesty, Emperor Showa of Japan. Some of the results of these meetings have been forwarded to me, and I believe that today is the best day for their communication. As you know, the first of the decisions of our two great and wise monarchs has come true here, this morning, with Hawaiians and Japanese both adopting the gods of the other, and thus becoming brother civilizations. This is symbolized by the erection of a *tori* here on Haleakalā. In a more secular, but no less meaningful gesture, King Kamāmalu and Emperor Showa have agreed that your Mauna Kea, and our Mt. Fuji, should be declared to be sister peaks. These mountains stand guard over the Pacific and the Greater East Asia Co-Prosperity Sphere. Both, in their perfection, symbolize the perfect order that is coming to pass here on earth, and both, in their volcanic nature, tell us that the result of a fiery beginning is a pure, unsullied land born of the sun, the earth, and the sea. Both mountains stand guard over empires that were created by farmers and warriors and that continue to have love of the earth and selfless sacrifice for the good of the many as their core values. For these reasons, let Mauna Kea and Fujisan stand, now and forever, for our new order!"

At that, some even clapped briefly, and a few heads dropped into prayerful postures for a few moments.

"In accordance with these first two steps, then, it is the duty of humankind to create a memorial to the world our gods and our mountains have given us. For that reason, your King Kamāmalu has graciously offered, and the emperor of Japan has agreed, to use the Bishop Museum as a center for Pacific studies, to continue to show both the glorious ancient past that we share, and to promote the study of the civilization that is now taking root. The museum will no longer concentrate on decadent Western natural science, but will commit itself and its resources to finding out more about how we are connected, and in which ways our various cultures interacted in the past. It is clear that we have much in common, from the similarity of our indigenous religious beliefs to our sea-based livelihoods. There must be links, long forgotten, between our civilizations in the past. The Bishop will find them and enlighten the world about the chosen of the gods. This way, the world will know how we Asians, together, were able to navigate the vast Pacific Ocean centuries before Europeans could even think of venturing into the Atlantic. The world will know how we, together, terrorized the Pacific coasts of China and Indochina with our bravery and skills in battle, before Europeans were even thinking of venturing beyond their own shores. We have triumphed, and the Bishop will show the world why. We will be the pinnacle of human evolution, and the Bishop will be our record book.

"In accordance with these things, it has also been decided

that that center of decadent, prideful skepticism, the University of Hawai'i, an American, and therefore Western institution, shall be closed. Its most deserving students will be offered an opportunity to study in Japan and take part in the development of that great enterprise of Japanese Science. Science with a spiritual base has made it possible for our military to sweep through Asia and will make you powerful as well. In order to maintain a working economy, the Honolulu Technical School will remain operational, to train workers for the daunting task ahead as Hawai'i joins Japan in creating the new world order. The University of Hawai'i, however, has no place in the order that is to be created. Its instructors and professors who are qualified and maintain the correct attitude toward their research, including a respect for the king of Hawai'i, the emperor of Japan, and the sacred nature of the earth, will be asked to come to Japan or to found new schools here in the islands. Most of the instructors at that cesspool of doubt and disorder, however, continue to think in the way they have been trained by their American government puppet-masters. They continue to doubt the divine origins of the Hawaiian and Japanese races. They cannot be reformed, and it would be a waste of money and time to try. They will be given safe conduct to a neutral zone where they can meet with representatives of the United States who will decide their fates. In this way, perhaps they can also help America understand the bankruptcy of her ways and the fait accompli that is the Greater East Asia Co-Prosperity Sphere. Thank you."

Mori bowed to the fifteen priests gathered in front of him and crisply stepped off the platform, watching eyes and calculating whether his latest effort to win the hearts of Hawai'i was going to work. These religious figures held sway with their followers. Their positive reports would go a long way toward providing the Japanese with credibility and legitimacy as defenders here.

Now to go on to phase two: undermining Christianity

among the Hawaiians so that more of them returned to their old ways. This would, he calculated, at once diminish the credibility of the Americans who had force-fed Christianity to these people in any case and increase the legitimacy of Japan here, since Shinto was so close to this indigenous religion. That was the hope. But things, he knew, rarely worked out as the planner hoped.

Stepping into his car, he wondered, as the engine fired, how careful he would have to be to keep this ball rolling in the direction he wanted. It helped, he supposed, that he believed that what he was saying was the truth. As long as he never lied to these people, he could win them over somehow—even if it was just with sincerity.

October 2, 1943. The road from Haleakalā

King Stephen Kamāmalu of Hawai‘i rode in a new Packard recently confiscated from the president of Alexander and Baldwin Co., the Big Five company that had controlled most of Maui until recently. The king was surprised and a bit angry at the luxury the car afforded. He looked at his advisor, an elderly *kahuna* named Kaleo Kekaula. "You know that Mori never really expects us to remain a kingdom."

"That, your majesty, is obvious."

"My chief concern is that we do. We must decide on a course of action that will help us use this Japanese 'restoration' of the kingdom to its nominal independent status as a step to gaining actual independence. How can we go about that?"

"Your majesty, whether Mori knows it or not, I think we have taken an important step here today. This dedication on top of Haleakalā brings notice to Hawaiian tradition. We must be careful, because, as you know, most Hawaiians are Christians, and while the Japanese wish to eradicate Christianity, I think we should recognize it as truth. Nevertheless, the interest today's ceremony brings is not so much in the traditional

Hawaiian religion, as it is in traditional Hawai'i. Among our native people, we should continue to promote remembrance of the traditional culture and traditional values of self-sufficiency and sacredness of place. These things are not incompatible with Christian beliefs, and are reinforced by our own ceremonies."

"I agree. We must begin to find a way to unify Hawaiians. But what do we do when the time comes to finally take our kingdom back? We have no army, and I will not fool myself into believing the Japanese will give us guns to use to rebel against them."

"No, you are correct there. This is a problem. If we allow the Americans to liberate Hawai'i from the Japanese, they will bring the Big Five back with them, and Hawai'i will once more be a territory of the United States. If we do not have the Americans to help, then where will we get the arms and the men? All of the answers will come in time. We must continue to keep our eyes open, and our minds ready to bend to the current situation. Perhaps the answer will present itself."

"For an advisor, I sometimes find you less concrete than I might hope. However, I suppose you are correct. Hasty decisions at this point could lead to many deaths and the total loss of what little we have gained so far. Please keep me posted on what you hear and see among the people."

"As you say, my king."

VOICES

25

Ted's Story: A Prisoner of War

August 22, 1943

Dear Flo,

I was late to roll call this morning. One of the Japanese officers, a young man with a limp—we called him gimpy—kicked my left shin so hard my leg slipped out from under me, and I fell. He grinned down at me and screamed in Japanese for a sergeant to discipline me, because in refusing to stand at attention, I was disrespecting the Japanese army, and therefore, the emperor. He said all this in Japanese, and I understood it, because my parents spoke Japanese. He then looked at me and said, in broken English, "You Japanese, but can not speak Japanese. You fighting Japanese army coming to freeing you. Must learn. Will teach."

Yoshida came and looked me over. The men now standing at attention behind me were silent, as I knew they must be, or receive the same treatment. Yoshida felt my arms, then hit me, hard, in the stomach. It was all I could do to remain upright and pretend to breathe normally, even though I felt like I was suffocating from uncontrollable muscle contractions in my abdomen. Yoshida looked impressed, and said to the officer,

"Judo." The officer nodded, and Yoshida took my arm and dragged me away.

I was strung up to a vertical pole by both wrists, right in the middle of the camp, where the sun was already beating down hard. All I had on was a dirty lavalava. I remember thinking how old my body looked to me. I waited for a very long time, sunburned, sweating, covered with flies, dangling from the pole with my toes barely touching the ground. When Yoshida came back, things got worse.

He cut me down with a slash from a knife. He told me if I flinched while he slashed, I would get worse punishment, so I stared straight ahead, praying the knife would cut the ropes and not my arms or wrists. Suddenly I felt a loss of tension and tumbled to the ground. But I knew the rules, and I used my still-bound hands to push myself upright immediately. Yoshida smiled. In a patronizing voice, certain I could not understand a word, he said, *"Kyō ha, ore no judō no renshuu aite ga o mae da."* (Today, you are my judo sparring partner.)

I didn't make a move, even when he cut the rope that bound my hands. He stepped in for a first hold. I knew that if I used the judo my father had taught me, and resisted or even prepared for the fall, he would work until he killed me. So I stood upright, acting stupid, and allowed him to grasp my lavalava at the waist, place his right foot behind mine, and push my upper torso until I fell. I knew how to fall, and I did a minimal fall to keep my breath and cushion my weakened back. I slapped the ground as I went down.

"Very good, *gaijin*," he said, as he stepped in with a cloth belt in his hands, which he wrapped around the back of my neck like a necktie. He twisted the belt around to the front and grasped it right at the nape of my neck. He slid his left hand under my left armpit, grasped the belt, and kept pressure on my sternum with the weight of his body on his left hand, which held me down. He looked into my eyes.

I could feel my lips turning blue, as I tried not to look desperate for air. Not struggling, but acting as if he was not—could not possibly be capable of—hurting me, was my last and only act of resistance to this man.

I woke up on my cot. They didn't take me to the sick bay. Bastards. I suppose they thought I was going to die, and didn't want it reported that I had been strangled. Better to let me die here, so it could be called "natural causes."

I'm still alive, though. I'll see you soon. Don't give in to these maniacs. God, I hope they are treating you all right. I wish you would just stop working here. It breaks my heart to think of you having to stand up to what I know these guards are capable of.

The longer I am in here, the more I know my choice to work for the resistance was right. The treatment of people in here, and in the islands in general, is horrible. How can we be Japanese and they be Japanese, too? They are more like demons than humans. Does Grandfather know they are like this?

Your brother,
Ted

VIGNETTES

26

The Death of an Old Soldier

March 15, 1945. Waikīkī Beach

General Mori walked slowly along the sand, just above the surf line, hands clasped behind his back. His booted feet made deep imprints in the wet sand. As he walked, he stared at the ocean, not contemplating, just staring. For the first time in three years, he was free of thoughts during his morning walk. That made him walk uncharacteristically slowly.

He walked his usual path: from the hotel he turned left as soon as he reached the beach, and walked its length. He usually went all the way to Diamond Head, threading his way through the American barbed wire.

Mori walked slowly because he'd been called home. With commendations, no less. He was going to be sent to the Imperial Army Headquarters, as an advisor on methods of pacifying local populations in the Pacific and making their territories productive and easier to operate for the Japanese Empire.

He'd already gone through the shock. The blood had drained from his face as he'd realized what a snake pit he was going to. He would be going back as a member of the Imperial Way faction of the army, to face the pencil-pushing administrators who headed the Control Faction. Even though they were of the same service, and served the same emperor, the methods of the two branches were as different as night and day. The Control Faction saw everything in cold, administrative terms. People weren't people for them, but statistics and pay accounts. Mori's own faction was dedicated to the emperor and to raising the Japanese nation into its rightful place in the world. This meant control of Asia, not only to exploit its resources, but also to create an orderly society based on the natural order of Asian peoples, with Japan at the top, and other Asians ranged below the Japanese according to their abilities and importance. Proper application of this policy meant that Imperial Way soldiers had to be men of action who could handle decisions quickly on the ground. They would do anything to achieve the mission. Controllers were much more interested in administrative "realities," and people came second to making sure the organization and supply structure were correct. They were an inflexible bunch of fools. And they were no doubt upset that Mori had been so successful.

Thinking this over, he'd reviewed his accomplishments in Hawai'i: a quick invasion, followed by the reestablishment of the Hawaiian monarchy and its incorporation into the scheme of the Greater East Asia Co-Prosperity Sphere. He had accomplished much and become a local hero to many of the Japanese and Hawaiians for his restoration of the monarchy and his redistribution of the land. He'd had to remind himself that those policies had been calculated to win popularity for himself and security for his troops. Nevertheless, many locals saw a good thing in this occupation. He'd been proud of his achievements and of their effectiveness in serving his emperor. Now he was going to be called home and taken to task because he had done exactly what he believed he was supposed to do—but in so doing had taken the wind out of the Control Faction's sails. Not only had they never fully backed the idea of occupying Hawai'i; they also saw it as contrary to their plan to control the continent of Asia. He would be punished for showing them it could be done, cheaply. Although he could see nothing dishonorable in serving his emperor well, he felt the ignominy that awaited him in Tokyo was a poor way to serve.

As he walked, he now thought of nothing. In a kind of pseudo Zen meditation, he cleared his mind of everything in preparation for his next task. Just as the *samurai* had been, he was resigned to his duty, whether that meant physical death or the much more agonizing political death he knew he would experience at Imperial Headquarters. His association before the war with the Imperial Way Faction of the army had angered others of his age from the Control Faction. He had refused to participate in the 1936 attempted coup in Tokyo, carried out by members of his own Imperial Way Faction. He had insisted, against the Imperial Way Faction wishes in 1931, that the Manchurian incident should be left to government negotiations. He'd opposed his own faction and upheld the positions of the Control Faction because he had thought peace might still achieve the goals of the emperor and the nation. Still he had earned the enmity of some very powerful people high up in the Control hierarchy. Those people apparently did not care much for his success here. He knew this was the end of his career, and quite possibly his life. He would much rather die on the battlefield than as an ostensible "advisor" whose duties would see every possible barrier put in his way until he could only fail despite his best efforts. Better even, he was thinking, to die the victim of an assassin's bullet than the victim of petty politics.

Mori was thinking this, ironically, at the very moment a bullet entered the base of his skull, severing his spinal column instantly and making his wish for assassination the last thought he had. The beach around him was, for the first and not the last time, red with human blood and scattered with brain tissue. The soldier had died a soldier's death.

March 30, 1945.
Luakini Heiau, above Waimea Bay, O'ahu

The king of Hawai'i, still scheming to keep his kingdom after the war ended, stood before a gathering of a few Japanese soldiers, a Shinto priest, and several Hawaiian *kāhuna* in ceremonial garb, including Kaleo Kekaula. All snapped to attention as the king stood, also wearing ceremonial costume, in the center of a large *luakini heiau*—a traditional Hawaiian war temple.

"This man," the king said, indicating the casket of General Mori, "saved us from ignominy," said the king. "His government and family have been kind enough to allow us to honor him by giving him a Hawaiian ceremony here and laying him to rest alongside the great kings and queens of Hawai'i in the Royal Mausoleum in Honolulu. I know they will welcome him, for he has given us the greatest of gifts. He has returned to us what was lost—ourselves and our islands. No longer will the kingdom of Hawai'i belong to another nation. No longer will others tell us how to behave, or what is important, or with whom we can consort. General Mori was always fair. He was the architect of Hawaiian freedom and independence, and we will always treasure his brief time here, regarding him as one sent by the gods to help our people reclaim what is theirs. It is fitting that he should be buried with our royalty."

At the king's words, flames were touched to the casket. It was a ceremony that was not traditionally held at a *luakini heiau*. The king had accepted the advice of Kekaula, who had himself suggested bending Hawaiian tradition. The point of this pseudo-traditional ceremony to honor Mori was, of course, not directed at the Japanese or at Mori's family at all. The goal was to give Native Hawaiians a focus for nationalism in the form of a man who had given them back their king. Mori represented the Japanese, who had temporarily liberated Hawai'i from occupation by the United States. This ceremony was designed to contribute to a refusal to accept reoccupation when the Americans finally drove the Japanese from Hawaiian shores.

VOICES

27

Ted's Story: On the Beach

April 1945

Dear Flo,

I'm writing to you about a day not so long ago. As was usual by 1945, I had no shirt on my back and I was feeling the trades in my hair and the familiar burn of the sun on my skin. Looking at the waves, I felt like having a swim, and looked at my companion, a *haole* named Ray, ready to ask if he was interested. I must've been delirious, because suddenly, looking at Ray's loose skin, wrinkled face, and thinning hair, I realized that neither of us could go for a swim. In fact, we probably couldn't even make it to the barbed wire lining the beach without being shot to death.

We were on a mission that could save hundreds of lives if we were successful. We were scouting for whatever the sea chose to give up that day, or in the week since a mission had gone out: dried seaweed, small shellfish, jellyfish left by the waves to die, dry, and rot on the sand.

Ray had come along at my suggestion. At least a hundred other guys volunteered. All of them deserved it. I got to choose because I had survived my fourth beating from Yoshida. My feet were swollen, since he had beaten them raw only a week before. They were still purple in some places, and too big for shoes—which was fine, since none of us had those, anyway.

But I had chosen Ray because he needed to get out of the camp. We all did. But Ray was closer to losing it than anyone else I knew. He claimed he could see clouds when there was nothing but blue sky. He commented on the beauty of the autumn leaves in the middle of May, in Hawai'i. He said he was planning to play mud football with his cousins on Thanksgiving.

We called it prison fever. Ray was slowly exchanging the reality of his POW life for the safety of his childhood in Maine. He'd been one of those prisoners who took the Japanese seriously when they castigated army survivors for having lived. The Japanese meant they had not given everything—including their lives—to the battle. Most of us saw things the way American culture did—that living to fight another day was a greater service to your country than dying futilely on a lost battlefield. But guys like Ray heard something else in the Japanese speech. They heard that survival was a disgrace, that perhaps their deaths could have saved the life of a friend, or more than one.

It never occurred to Ray, as it often did to me, that maybe those guys who died fighting off the Japanese invasion were better off than we were. They didn't have to deal with this camp. In fact, if he had saved their lives, we tried to point out to him, they might have cursed him for it because it would have landed them in the Frying Pan.

But Ray didn't buy this. He saw it as his solemn duty to escape at any cost, at first, and tried several different things. All he got for it were beatings, and once he was even made to "dance," western movie style, while the group commander of the Japanese fired bullets into the ground near his feet.

Now he was away from that, if only briefly. I thought bringing him out of the wire, into beauty and free space, might help him. It wasn't working. He was walking with me, but I had to do all the hunting for food. I picked up my bucketful, then his bucketful. The Japanese guard thankfully didn't say anything when I changed buckets with him. There was just no covert way to do it.

Then, just a few minutes before we reached the spot where we would turn inland to walk back to the camp, Ray broke. I should never have had him out there. He dropped his bucket, and I, thinking of the food, bent down to put everything back in. He ran for the wire and the sea and, I suppose, freedom.

Our guard didn't bat an eyelash. He simply raised his rifle and fired into Ray's back. Five times. Momentum carried Ray forward, probably still conscious, until he stepped on a land mine, set there by the Americans to defend against a possible Japanese invasion—and left by the economical Japanese army.

His body was everywhere. A foot dropped on my shoulder, and I, in near panic, brushed it off as I would a poisonous spider, then kicked it away. The sand where he had been was cratered a bit, and dark, since the wet sand beneath the surface had been blown out. His large intestine unraveled in the waves twenty-five feet down the beach, and bobbed as fish nibbled at it. A severed hand lay in the foreground, its fingers clenched tightly in the fist of a runner. I looked down, careful not to see anything else as I collected my buckets and kept walking. I wanted to be sick, and I wanted to weep. But I also wanted to live. Now, more than ever.

It was awful, Flo. I hope that you are doing all right. I think about you every day. Please be okay.

Ted

VIGNETTES

28
Kimura's Revenge

April 1945

Lieutenant Kimura said quietly, "We have to make an example of someone to show that we will not take this cowardly assassination and these acts of sabotage lying down."

He was speaking to General Yasushi Kamata and to Kamata's chief aid, Lieutenant Nakasone, in a meeting in General Mori's old office. His voice was quivering with emotion, and Nakasone thought one might even believe Kimura was filled with righteous indignation and grief for his commander. He would have believed it if he didn't already know Kimura's reputation for cruelty. A reformer to the end, Mori had taken Kimura under his wing with the intent of reforming him. Nearly every Japanese officer in the Pacific had heard of Kimura's exploits. He had been everywhere the Japanese army was, and everywhere he had instigated cruel treatment of prisoners or locals. He was, no doubt about it, a sadist. He enjoyed torture, and was said to have spent twenty minutes twisting a knife in the abdomen of a prisoner in China, just so that he could study the man's eyes as he died. Nakasone knew that Kimura wanted both command responsibility and satisfaction of his cruel fantasies. In this case, Nakasone knew he was likely to get both. Strange how the pathways of chance met up in this world.

Nakasone said, "Be civil in front of General Kamata."

"It's all right," the general said. "Clearly this young man is grieving for a beloved mentor. I agree with him. We must show these people they cannot play with us. What do you suggest, Lieutenant?"

Nakasone knew Kamata was playing Kimura for a fool. But they had to let the local population know that assassination of Japanese officers was not tolerated. If they used Kimura's suggestion, he could be put in command, and any mistakes or problems later encountered could be laid at Kimura's feet should they prove insoluble.

"You honor me, general, with the question. I suggest we arrest representatives of those we think are committing these crimes against us. It need not be the actual perpetrators. Just those they might know. Or better, those who are friends and family of people who might know the saboteurs and will plead with them to stop when they see their families suffer. These people we should display in some public area, perhaps the palace, as they receive punishment—I suggest public whippings, or perhaps the beating and burning of the soles of their feet. This should put pressure on the saboteurs to stop."

Kamata spoke. "Kimura, you are right that we need not get the saboteurs themselves. In fact, we may be more effective by causing the pain to friends and relatives. However, you must learn more caution, my boy. If we, the Japanese liberators of Hawai'i, string them up at the palace and carry out the torture in public, much of our credibility will be lost. We will have desecrated the ground that is now so holy to Native Hawaiians and, in the process, shown outright who holds the real power of law and order here.

"No, Kimura, we cannot torture in public, or we will risk making new saboteurs out of those who currently sit the fence. But we can start a fire—an accident. Those we most want to make an example of are the Chinese and the Filipino communities. They are the most likely sources of the violence. They have no reason to love Japan either here or in their homelands. While they may not be the only saboteurs, they are the only groups safe for us to accuse at this moment. These are your orders, Kimura: first, send a squad to comb Chinatown. Take every girl between the ages of fourteen and eighteen. Our men need more female companionship, and since the Chinese are not voluntarily helping out, they will be given a job. More comfort women, Kimura. No time for good-byes or packing. The women are to be taken out of the homes you find them in.

"Second, a serious fire must start in Waipahu. That is where most of the Filipinos in Honolulu live. The fire must become very large—so large, in fact, that we can send firefighting assistance, but it will be no help. I want all the houses to burn to the ground. The fire must appear to be an accident. And it must be so large and hot that all the firefighting forces on the island cannot challenge it. That should cause sufficient sorrow to stamp down these sabotage efforts for some time. We can then, quietly, finish our investigations and cause the real culprits to disappear."

"It will be as you say," barked Kimura, as he turned sharply on his heels and marched out the door. Kamata put the sorrow out of his head by lighting a cigar. What must be done, he thought, must be done. Expensive sabotage was wasteful, and the Japanese war machine was already stretched beyond its limits. It had been from day one. There was no money for repairs, and he was on an outpost that provided no raw materials for the empire. By later this year, when surplus production was forecast for most of the new territories, Hawai'i might get more men, more food, more gasoline. For now, he had to run Hawai'i on less than a shoestring budget, without Mori to shelter him from shame at every supply request he made to the home islands. He was expected to be self-sufficient. And he would be, or die trying. He turned back to the paperwork on his desk.

April 1945. Chinatown, Honolulu

The four soldiers smiled at each other. This was possibly the most interesting day of their tour here in Hawai'i so far. The lieutenant had said get the job done, and teach the Chinese a lesson doing it. They got together before departure and decided just how this lesson would go.

The first of them knocked on doors. They had no idea who lived where, but it didn't matter. If there were any young women in the apartment, they rounded them up—after giving them a taste of the job they would be performing from now on.

Some, the really quick-thinking ones, submitted right away. They tried to save their families the pain and humiliation by making things as quick and easy as possible. It was never easy, though, and some of the soldiers were angered when a woman took away their steam by being submissive. They got even more violent then.

This girl was one of those. She even forced a smile when they came in the door and found her sitting demurely on the sofa. Before they could say a word, she went into a room off the main one. They followed. She had a bag ready. She picked it up, making ready to go. She motioned to the door.

One of the soldiers grabbed her arm, roughly, and pulled her to his face. He smiled greedily. She lost her smile, then. In Japanese he said, "Best to test the wares before you buy."

She looked confused, but then quickly smiled again as he threw her on the floor. She lifted the hem of her dress and motioned him to come to her. But she lost her composure and screamed when all of them started to move, with wolfish grins on their faces, and the first soldier pulled out his service knife.

When she did come out of the apartment, twenty minutes later, she was not walking, and she knew she had been wrong to think she could protect herself by acting. Her shell had been totally destroyed, and she cried for her mother and father as she was pulled through the door, breaking her last nail below the quick on the doorjamb as she tried to hold on to her home, her family, her past, her self.

Late August 1945. Waipahu, O'ahu

It was a humid night, and the trades had stopped blowing. It was the kind of night when all chicken skin stories are scarier, and nothing seems normal. It was the perfect night for a witching, and that was what seemed to be happening.

The old Filipino men, out on porches talking story before bed, saw the torches first. Hundreds of them appeared at the top of the hill, like jewels, and entranced their watchers. The whisper started in one of the small whitewashed houses, and ran like a wind down the hill toward the harbor. This was horrible beauty. The old men knew. Waipahu was being set afire.

Hawai'i's Filipino community had been outspoken in their anti-Japanese sentiment and actions. They'd heard, from cousins, grandparents, friends at home, over hidden ham radios, what the Japanese had done on the Bataan Peninsula and how people were being treated there. A fire this big left no doubt what was going on. The Japanese were taking retribution for the community's sabotage and other acts of resistance.

The whisper sent people fleeing in to wake up children, get them dressed, and pack food if possible. People were in the streets, but they knew they couldn't go up into the saddle between the two O'ahu mountain ranges. Within fifteen minutes of the appearance of the torches, the fire had already grown huge, licking the stars with its orange tips, burning the twelve-foot-high cane fields in a maelstrom that many would later call their image of hell. It was impossible to imagine moving through that firestorm. Most ran to Pearl Harbor, pushing others into the water before them. Men, women, and children drowned, exhausted from swimming so long or pulled down in the general panic.

By morning, all that was left of the Filipino community in

Waipahu was ashes, a pair of reading glasses here, a singed doll there. Five hundred people had drowned. Others who escaped the blaze made it safely down the valley or over to the windward side.

Leaders of the survivors complained to the government of King Kamāmalu. The government responded that it had sent all the firefighters it had, but the conflagration was already out of control. Asked where the Japanese army was, General Kamata responded that he would have sent troops to help, but most were on maneuvers in other areas and did not arrive until after the fire had burned itself out. He did volunteer to have his army help pick up the bodies of the dead and deliver them to a mass burial pit that had been prepared for "sanitary" reasons.

VIGNETTES

29
Midway Blast

August 6, 1945

The skies above Midway Atoll were a bright blue. Far north and east of the island of Oʻahu, where General Mori, until his death, and now General Yasushi Kamata, were continuing to integrate the Hawaiian Islands into the empire of Japan, this farthest reach of the Hawaiian chain was experiencing a peaceful dawn.

The current inhabitants of Midway included several hundred sea birds, a contingent of one thousand Japanese army regulars to man defenses, and a few technical and administrative personnel from the Japanese Imperial Navy, whose job it was to operate the atoll as a way station, fueling depot, and listening post. This was an operational base, and though not nearly as big as Oʻahu, it was Japan's closest link with the farthest western reaches of its empire, which now covered nearly a full quarter of the surface of the globe. The Midway operatives were, understandably, proud of their position and of the empire they had helped Japan to win and gain. They also felt sure the United States had given up on its Pacific possessions. That had been clear almost since the 1942 invasion of Hawaiʻi.

Since February 1942, the United States had clearly slunk back into its den in San Diego and did not intend to challenge Japanese supremacy in Asia. In December of '41, the great carrier *Enterprise* had sunk, along with most of the battleships of its Pacific Fleet. What remained of that force had been confined to Pearl Harbor by the sunken hulk of *Enterprise* herself. The *Lexington*, badly damaged by Japanese bombs, had been seen limping back to San Diego, and *Saratoga*, the one remaining Pacific carrier, was left without escort or ground support for any sorties into the great ocean. Furthermore, since the success of the invasion, the United States had not been heard from in the Pacific.

Almost not heard from. The soldiers and sailors on Midway had no way to know of continued diplomatic rumblings from Washington, since all official diplomatic contact had been cut off even before Roosevelt's "Day of Infamy" speech beseeching Congress to declare war on Japan. They had heard, through indirect channels, of a few sorties into the Pacific since Germany's defeat in the spring of 1945, but still could not believe there was any threat to the empire.

This was the exact course the Americans' by now well known War Plan Rainbow Five had set. Until the war in Europe was finished, the United States would go on the defensive in the Pacific and concentrate on Europe. So far, there were no murmurings that the United States had now shifted its focus of operations, and the Japanese believed that silence meant the United States was going to give in and leave the Pacific to Japan.

They did concede grudging admiration to the United States for its role in defeating Japan's erstwhile ally, Germany. No matter now, their commanders told them. The alliance was no longer necessary. Japan's empire was established. This year, 1945, some real profit was being made by the empire. Oil was flowing more freely from Indochina. Rubber, iron, and gold were making their way from the East Indies more quickly, now that time and steel could be spent on manufacturing merchant ships. Japan, said the officers, could stand alone now.

However strong the Europeans had seemed, they were at heart soft, because they did not have spirit like the Japanese. They were not descendants of Amaterasu, the sun goddess, and they did not have the steel will to serve a divine and benevolent emperor. The Japanese Empire was a fact, and strategically impregnable.

So the sun rose on a vigilant but confident group of a little over one thousand men ashore on Midway. Three carriers, *Zuikaku*, *Shokaku*, and *Kaga*, along with their escorts, had arrived the previous day from Japan. Their purpose was to take on fuel, then continue a patrol of the North Pacific. No incidents were expected. The Pacific was now a Japanese lake.

That was why, at just after 6:32 a.m., air reconnaissance was so surprised to sight a single, two-engine plane. The airfield controllers checked their logs and noted that no planes were due in at that time, and certainly none with two engines. The carrier air patrol (CAP) planes—sentries guarding the air space around the carriers—went to take a look, and from several hundred yards out confirmed that this was not a Japanese craft. It looked distinctly American and matched the drawings they had been shown of a B-29 bomber. They'd never expected to see one here, they thought, as they moved in for the attack.

As the CAPs came within range of its guns, the B-29 began shooting back from nearly every imaginable place on its fuselage. It took out two planes before help could arrive, and continued on its course—one that would take it directly over Midway and the carrier force.

Five of the latest Mitsubishi Zero fighters scrambled from the deck of *Shokaku*, the closest carrier to the action, as a few older models trundled off the airfield on the atoll. All headed straight for the bomber and were caught by surprise when ten American fighters came out of the sunrise in the east to engage them before they reached their quarry.

August, 6, 1945, 6:34 a.m.
Above Midway Atoll

"They probably can't believe their eyes," thought Colonel Fitzpatrick, commander and pilot of *Doolittle's Brainchild*. The B-29 was named after Colonel Doolittle, who had begun planning a raid on Tokyo immediately after the Japanese had bombed Pearl Harbor in 1941. Doolittle had moved up in rank and on to bigger jobs since then. With no Hawai'i, the U.S. Navy had deemed it too risky to send a carrier battle group into unfriendly waters for what would essentially be a symbolic act, with little chance of causing major damage. But Fitzpatrick had been one of the pilots Doolittle had used in his experiments with flying the bombers off a carrier.

Today, however, Fitzpatrick and his crew had staged out of a special base in the Aleutian Island chain off Alaska. The place was perfect for the mission, with reinforced concrete hangers dug into the side of a rugged mountain. The base was all safety. *Doolittle's Brainchild* had been the only aircraft on the base today. It certainly would not be the only one there when it returned. After this mission, the whole damned Army Air Force would probably be there. If they got back at all.

"First, gotta fly through this muck." He couldn't believe his eyes, either. Four years of War Plan Rainbow Five had apparently given the enemy a case of overconfidence. He hadn't been seen until he was well within view of his target. His eyes lit up when he saw the three carriers, in close, packed together to get their gas. Just before he was sighted, he had given his radioman the message to send to the *Saratoga* battlegroup: "Got the tiger by the tail." It was an oblique reference to the Japanese message, since decoded and isolated, that Fuchida had sent on December 7, 1941, to the Japanese battle group: *Tora, tora, tora*—tiger, tiger, tiger. Its meaning wasn't clear. The meaning of Fitzpatrick's message was simple: "arrived safely, beginning run."

The run would not be a cakewalk, he realized, as antiaircraft guns got in on the act from the islands on the ring that was Midway. That buffeted the air a bit, but for this mission, he was high enough not to be too worried. It was the fighters that had his nerves a-jangle. Them, and the cargo he carried.

The Zeros looked within range when suddenly his escort appeared out of the sun almost directly ahead. Just ten. All modified P-51 Mustangs, developed for the war against Germany. These had folding wings, and wing tanks to increase their range, and more powerful engines—all designed to make them carrier aircraft, which, he noted, like his clunker, they still really were not. He wished his own country knew something about how these Zeros were built.

He had to stay on course at twelve thousand feet—a difficult job for his craft. He was near flight ceiling now and, well, even with new, high accuracy bombsights also developed in the war against Germany, he was glad he wouldn't need to be very accurate. He concentrated on the target.

With the air alive around him, the heat of a warming day, the turbulence from ack-ack, the tracers and, he knew, bullets from those trying to shoot him down, he passed command to his bombardier, who began directing the airplane right down the alley toward the carriers. Fitzpatrick could see more planes leaving their decks, ready to defend the mother's womb from which they were born, and to which they retreated after battle. Each pilot, he knew, was experienced, both in battle, and with his aircraft. This would not be easy.

As the bombardier called bay doors open, a lone Zero moved into range, evading the six Mustangs left in the air. Fitzpatrick resisted the urge to jink, and kept on course, but told the gunners where to look. Tracers flew around him. The Zero stayed glued to him.

At 0 minus 30 seconds, the Zero scored a hit on his left engine.

Slowed to less than optimum speed, and struggling now to

keep his altitude above twelve thousand feet, Fitzpatrick grimly stayed on course. He saw a Mustang spin toward the sea, on fire, a wing missing—and heard the pilot scream on the radio link. "Stay on course," he thought. Thirty seconds was an eternity.

When it elapsed, time and sound seemed to vanish. At nearly the same moment, a large, fat cylinder with four fins, painted black, dropped from the bomb bay of the B-29, and the tail rudder was shredded, causing Fitzpatrick to lose yaw control and sending the aircraft into an almost controllable horizontal spin. Concentrating on control, Fitzpatrick was unable to maintain altitude.

August 6, 1945, 2:40 a.m. Tokyo, Japan

The signal came in from the *Shokaku*, flagship for Admiral Nagumo on his latest Pacific perimeter cruise: engaging unknown flight group, one bomber, ten fighter aircraft, possibly American, over Midway. Strange configuration, and the presence of only . . .

The message ended, and only static followed. Knowing how weather and battle can interfere with communications, the navy high command was pensive, but not particularly concerned, and waited twenty-four hours before sending urgent requests for communication to Nagumo. None were answered.

August 6, 6:40 a.m. Midway Atoll

The flash was blinding as the A-bomb went off at just over one hundred feet above the water. With the core of the explosion hotter than the surface of the sun, a heat wave rode the shock wave outward and upward and obliterated everything around it in a two-mile radius. *Shokaku*, *Zuikaku*, and *Kaga*, though they gallantly remained afloat for several hours after the explosion, were burning hulks that shared perhaps fifty living bodies among them, out of more than six thousand at sunrise. Those living did not stay that way for long, and several used their remaining strength to hasten their departure—and the relief of the pain, blindness, and near madness they felt. Most couldn't move, though, because before the blast, out of some instinct, they had taken shelter behind solid steel fixtures on their ships. They couldn't move, not because metal had fallen on them, but because the intensity of the heat wave had melted them to their cover. It was agonizing, and the pain of saltwater filling their seared lungs as the carriers and their escorts went down was almost welcomed by many of those who experienced it.

The fleet was gone. So was all superstructure on Midway. The shock wave had flattened Quonset huts and buildings, sent sandbags from gun emplacements into the air to shower their radioactive contents on everything around, poisoning the island. The few trees, and the sea birds that had nested in rocks and on sand, near and around the trees, were swept away in a wind that made most recent hurricanes look like a spring breeze.

The *Doolittle's Brainchild* spiraled down into the maelstrom her cargo had created, and Fitzpatrick had no time to watch as his plane was ripped apart by the force of the rising mushroom cloud. Fighting the control stick, he didn't even have time to know he was about to die. Within seconds he, his crew, and the airplane were obliterated by the most powerful force ever unleashed by humankind. They were not to know that America's first serious strike in the war against Japan had been a blinding success.

A lone P-51 pilot knew, and radioed that information to the *Saratoga* battle group, along with his own position, fifty miles southwest of the disaster, just before he had to ditch his plane because he'd run out of fuel protecting the most terrible thing he'd ever seen. As he flew toward the waves in the silence of a feathered propeller, he knew this was the beginning of more killing. But payback had been made for Pearl Harbor, and there seemed to be justice in that.

The pilot pulled the inflator tab on his life jacket and ejected just before his plane hit the water. With luck, his rubber boat would inflate, and he'd be found.

VISTAS

30
Gyokusai Honolulu:
The Smashing of the Jewels

Good afternoon. By the spring of 1945, the war in Europe was over, and the United States turned its full attention to Japan. Japanese resolve can be seen in the following directive to the troops.

(October 1945)

"Soldiers and Sailors of his Imperial Majesty's Hawai'i Defense Force:

The military situation has entered its decisive phase. All of our efforts up to now will soon be put to the test. With the sudden and unexplained disappearance of the Hawai'i-based naval force and garrison at Midway, we have become the first line of defense for the Japanese home islands. We believe the Americans have used some kind of super bomb in a surprise attack at Midway. There were reports of a single blinding flash from the direction of Midway, followed by one long thunderous roar. That is all, then silence and static. In any case, this weapon will do the Americans no good here on heavily populated O'ahu. The marines will have to wade ashore, into our guns.

162

Just as the *samurai* of the Kamakura Shogunate pushed the Mongol barbarians back into the sea, so shall we do this with the Western barbarians, avenging their unwanted intrusion with Perry in 1854. Every man will do his duty; sell your lives dearly for the emperor. *Banzai.*"

After the nuclear destruction of the main Japanese Fleet at Midway, the radioactive atoll became the staging area for the assault on Oʻahu. Three carrier task forces massed—at San Francisco, San Diego, and Seattle—and formed up one thousand miles east of Hawaiʻi. American carrier-based aircraft now contested control of the skies with the Japanese land-based fighters on Oʻahu. The blue skies over the islands were filled with dozens of planes at any given time—Hellcats and Corsairs slugging it out with Zeros or "Zekes" based at Hickam/Nagumo Field and the upgraded Bellows Field. The air battle of Oʻahu raged for days, the people below witnessing an epic struggle of fighter aircraft at close range. At the higher altitudes, the staccato fire of the machine guns followed the trail of smoke and fire that erupted from the tail of the pursued planes, then the thickening plume of black smoke as the losers plunged toward the sea or augured into the Koʻolaus. Now that the Hawaiian Islands were isolated by the American Fleet based at Midway, the fleet's superior weight of numbers and arms could be brought to bear on the limited and dwindling Japanese air forces over Hawaiʻi. One by one, the outer islands were isolated and their Japanese garrisons wiped out. A second American military build-up began on Maui.

A lone H6K Mavis naval reconnaissance plane was the first to see the awesome sight—the U.S. Assault Force, which appeared on the western horizon. Comprising twenty-one carriers, ten battleships, one hundred destroyers carrying one hundred thousand troops of the 3d Marine Amphibious Corps and 24th Army Corps, this was the largest invasion force ever assembled in the Pacific up to that time. (The force assaulting

Okinawa three years later, in 1948, would be nearly double that size.) The American invasion began with a heavy artillery bombardment of the 'Ewa plains and coastal defenses, which were not yet lined with the heavy concrete bunkers and permanent artillery emplacements. SB2C Helldivers and Dauntless dive bombers made short work of the surviving guns and batteries along the 'Ewa coast, where the main invasion force came ashore. Streams of amphibious landing craft poured ashore along the entire eight-mile coast from Barbers Point to the channel entrance of Pearl Harbor. This was the least defended coast along O'ahu's shore, and seventy thousand troops established a beachhead and rapidly wheeled south, enveloping Pearl and Hickam in a wide arc. Behind the infantry came the tanks and mobile artillery as the American forces spread out over the 'Ewa plains.

Retreating Japanese forces demolished the docks, dry docks, hangers, and repair facilities at Pearl Harbor and Hickam Field as they moved toward Honolulu seeking better ground to make a stand. To block the rapidly advancing American troops, the Japanese rear echelon set afire the blocks of two-story wooden buildings of Iwilei and Chinatown. The bordellos, tattoo parlors, fish markets, *lei* stands, bars, dance halls, and food stalls were quickly transformed into a towering wall of flames, separating the retreating Japanese troops from the pursuing American forces. The terrified residents of Chinatown fled toward the mountains and harbor to get out of the raging inferno and away from the converging Japanese and American forces. Within a few hours, all that remained of Chinatown and its rich history was a smoldering pile of charred timber and twisted metal.

The destruction had served its purpose, however, as the Japanese were now securely entrenched in the multistoried steel and concrete buildings of downtown Honolulu, including the Hawaiian Electric Co. building, the Central Post Office, the Big Five office buildings of Castle and Cooke, American Factors, and the others. City Hall and the library were now heavily armed fortresses. The Armed Forces YMCA, ʻIolani Palace and the barracks became centers of Japanese resistance. The front line of Japanese defenders holding up the American advance was anchored at the Dole Cannery complex and Bishop Museum in Kalihi, while on the far side of downtown Honolulu, troops fortified the Judiciary Building and Territorial Office Buildings. Downtown Honolulu resembled the concentric rings of defenses in the old Japanese castles.

In the meantime, the thirty thousand troops of the second wave of the American invasion force came ashore at Waikīkī. In the interests of keeping good relations with the local population (and perhaps because of overconfidence), the Japanese had confined their defense efforts to underwater beach obstacles: steel beams driven into the reef and mounted with mines or steel-cutter "can openers" to impale landing craft, and naval mines anchored to the bottom farther out. They had even removed the ugly, useless strands of barbed wire that laced Waikīkī Beach during the earlier American defensive operations. Before the first assault waves came ashore, underwater demolition teams had blown up the obstacles and mines, and the American troops stormed ashore. They were met at the beach by Japanese defenders firing from hastily dug trenches and foxholes in the sand. The first waves of the assault forces came ashore at low tide, their landing craft hung up at the coral reefs, and they were forced to wade ashore in the shallow waters, into the withering machine-gun fire of the defenders. Soon the blue-green water off Waikīkī ran red with blood and filled up with floating bodies, but the advance could not be stemmed. Mortars opened up on the exposed Japanese positions, and plumes of sand gracefully shot upward following the muffled "whump" of the mortar shell explosion. Body parts also careened into the air. The Moana Hotel was engulfed in flames as Japanese defenders were flushed out and cut down. The Royal Hawaiian Hotel was reduced to a mass of pink rubble to affect the same end.

American forces now surrounded downtown Honolulu from three sides. They paused to regroup and coordinate their movements. When all was ready, the noose around the city was tightened as American troops converged down the main avenues of advance: down King, Dillingham, Beretania, and Vineyard, and up Ala Moana, King, and Beretania from Waikīkī; and from the *mauka* side, down Nuʻuanu, the Pali Highway, and Fort Street. The Japanese defenders were pressed from all sides, and they contested every building, every street as they were driven inward to the city center. There were numerous small unit actions all around the perimeter. Floor by floor, building by building, the Japanese defenders were cleared. The crackle of small arms fire echoed down the streets. In some of the more heavily built and massively defended buildings, the American attackers brought up tanks, heavy mortars, and 155-mm guns, firing them point-blank into the structures. Entire buildings were reduced to rubble, and the business district largely obliterated. As the Japanese troops saw their cause was hopeless, order and discipline collapsed. Hundreds of civilians caught in the crossfire were victims of torture, rape, and summary executions over the next two weeks.

There were savage firefights on the periphery of the city—the storming of the Kamehameha Schools complex on Kapalama Heights, the Bishop Museum "castle" battle. And there was the Punchbowl "last stand," where hundreds of Japanese soldiers retreated and defended against repeated assaults. They were finally overcome by precision napalm bombing, which incinerated them. That night, the Punchbowl Crater was a giant flaming bowl of fire. It looked as if the extinct volcanic crater had returned to life, spewing forth blood and lava. The thousands of bodies of Japanese soldiers were carted to the crater and cremated in a deep pit with their brothers in death. Honolulu, the Jewel of the Pacific, was again in American hands, but smashed beyond recognition.

VOICES

31
Flo's Story: A Nurse's Tale

Just as I'll never forget the day Pearl Harbor was bombed, I'll never forget the day Hawai'i was liberated by the United States.

It was an ambivalent liberation—especially for those of us in the Japanese community here. Most of us had been shocked at the brutality of the Japanese army. Our Japanese ancestry didn't prevent us from resisting the Japanese occupation. My brother Ted was among those who did fight the Japanese. Yet the fact that Japan controlled so much territory, and the way that General Mori restored the Hawaiian king and redistributed the land, made us feel that Japan wasn't all bad. We all hoped that some sort of Japan-America peace treaty would let Hawai'i become independent and end the war without more bloodshed.

We hoped for a future Hawai'i without outside control. Working with Hawaiians and Filipinos and Chinese in the resistance helped us feel we were a part of Hawai'i. I remember my father and grandfather telling stories about reaching a point in their lives when they, also, finally felt they belonged here. Perhaps this was that time for most of us, the younger generation.

So when the Americans returned, we weren't completely

sure we wanted them here—though by that time, the demands of the Japanese military had made life so brutal we were happy to be rid of them.

But not all of us were happy to see Japan defeated. There were probably as many "loyalists" among the Japanese in Hawai'i as their were those who resisted the occupation. My grandfather, who by choice never got his American citizenship, was one of the loyalists. When the final surrender of the Japanese troops was announced, he dug up a pistol he'd hidden away at the beginning of the war. He went out behind his house, placed a small straw mat on the ground and, dressed in the white of ritual purity, shot himself in the temple. I found him that way when I returned from the women's clinic that night.

My grandfather had been the rock in my world since the occupation of Hawai'i had begun. His kindness, his humanity, and his willingness to stand up to Japanese soldiers had given me reason to believe that his culture—my heritage—was not the cruelty I saw around me. I had been aware of the intense pride he felt with the successes of the empire, and of his desire to one day return to Kyushu, to his native village, to see what was left of his family and friends before he died. I had not expected this.

I remember crying as I covered him with another straw mat (I had used all of our white sheets for bandages). This war had taken nearly everything from me: Mother was killed in the Japanese invasion; Father and Ted were still alive, but at odds with each other over Ted's joining the resistance. Father had accepted land from the Japanese in the redistribution. Ted had been anxious to prove himself an American. I could understand both sides, but neither of them could see beyond his own nose, and so I had no family to gather together.

After the surrender, at the opening of the Diamond Head POW camp, I helped certify the health of the prisoners as they were identified and freed. I hugged my brother as he came through the infirmary and was thankful he was one of those who had family here. Many of the prisoners had been left behind in the evacuation of the island before the invasion, and now would have to sail to California on a hospital ship and from there travel overland to Oklahoma or Pennsylvania or Washington or other states before being reunited with loved ones.

The whole day was wonderful and awful. The men were free, but they looked gaunt, tired, barely alive. But the eyes of those who made it gave up their secret. Their eyes showed a refusal to die. Conditions that killed most people simply were not allowed, by force of will, to take these lives. I was amazed, and so, so happy to see Ted walk into the infirmary under his own power. I had no idea he would immediately volunteer to join the U.S. Army, or that such a move would lead to his death, only a few hundred meters from the village where our grandfather was born.

VISTAS

32
Last Stand at the Hirohito Line

I would like to begin this lecture with a statement by an American chaplain. The military initiative had clearly shifted to the United States.

(December 1945)

"Boys, we'll be landing soon. You already know the significance of what we're about to do. This is the first real piece of American soil we will take back from the Japs since their sneak attack here three years ago. We have had to leave four hundred thousand of Hawai'i's people, many of them American citizens, in the hands of those yellow bastards. We know from reports and actions elsewhere—Nanking, Hong Kong, Singapore, and the Philippines—that the Japs have done some pretty awful things to soldiers and civilians alike. Be prepared for some real bad things. May God bless you and protect you."

After the pincer movement around Honolulu, which, unfortunately, had to destroy the city to save it, American forces regrouped and proceeded down both the windward and leeward coasts of Oʻahu, on either side of the Koʻolaus, toward East Oʻahu and the concentrated Japanese defenses centered on Koko Crater. Japanese troops in Waimānalo moved up the narrow road past Makapuʻu Beach and up the other side near Koko Head, occupying the many caves, bunkers, and tunnel complexes prepared long before, well provisioned, well hidden, and well defended. Behind them streamed thousands of Japanese immigrant settlers, fearing rape and torture at the hands of the Americans. Death, they had been told, would be their fate if they tried to surrender. The main road, Kamehameha Highway, was blown up above the beach at Makapuʻu, and similarly closed on the slope above the heavily mined marshland before Koko Crater. Here they waited, behind the strongest defenses in the Pacific.

The minefields and tank traps took their toll on American troops and equipment; with a low, thudding sound, the mines sent trucks and men spiraling into the air. Slowly, laboriously, the mines and traps were cleared, and metal tracks were rolled across the marsh to make corduroy roads. The Japanese had mounted heavy artillery in the heights and on Koko Crater and Koko Head. They held their fire until the American attackers were only five hundred yards away. They then opened up with a barrage that decimated their ranks and drove them back beyond the marsh. For the next three days, American naval guns and heavy and light bombers took turns pounding the suspected positions, so well hidden by their builders. Again, infantry units started forward, only to be stopped in their tracks by hidden machine gun emplacements and long-range artillery that had their range. On the Makapuʻu side, with the road completely gone, troops tried to scramble up the steep slope that funneled to a point above the beach lookout over Rabbit Island. Hidden caves riddled the cliffside, and from these, snipers and machine gun crews picked off individual soldiers or mowed down whole squads proceeding single file up the face of the cliff. Some soldiers leapt off the side and took their chances in a fall rather than be potted like rabbits or squirrels in the deadly crossfire.

Slowly, painfully, the American assault forces worked their way forward. Each cave had to be located, isolated, and blown up or sealed shut. The tactic of using flamethrowers and explosives against caves was nicknamed the "blowtorch and corkscrew" as American troops worked their way up the Makapu'u side of the Hirohito Line, the thousands of Japanese civilian settlers brought to Hawai'i in the last year of the occupation massed on the steep cliffs.

One by one, in family groups, then by the dozens, they began to leap from the cliffs, falling hundreds of feet below onto the sharp rocks or the crashing surf, despite the entreaties of the American soldiers, horrified to see mothers jump with babes in their arms, fathers pushing their young sons, and with tears in their eyes, following them in death. Soon the seas and the shores of East O'ahu were littered with the floating corpses of these needless dead. Later in the war, this leap was repeated off Suicide Cliff on Saipan.

The Japanese planners had designed a zone of defense in depth, with the main stronghold of Koko Crater surrounded by a series of concentric rings of ever more deadly ingenuity. The defensive positions of machine gun posts and small bunkers and caves were mutually reinforcing, and Koko Crater itself was planned with cross-fire zones on both the forward and reverse slopes. The many gullies that furrowed the side of the crater afforded splendid opportunities for creating "Yankee death traps" as they called them. Whole squads of advancing soldiers were caught in the cross-fire zones and cut to pieces, not a man escaping. The next unit would hear the rapid firing and shouting, and by the time they arrived to help, there would just be a pile of corpses to greet them. A single day's advance through the "death zone" might be just forty yards!

Gradually, however, the overwhelming firepower of the American armed forces began its lethal attrition of the Japanese defenders. One by one, the big guns were located and destroyed, then the smaller artillery pieces on down to machine gun posts. The most dramatic example of this procedure was the positioning of the battleship *Missouri* close to the seaward slope of Koko Crater. Her massive 16-inch guns, with their 2,700-pound shells, fired point-blank into the crater walls, tearing out great chunks of lava rock and concrete bunkers. The crater wall became so pockmarked that it resembled the face of the moon. This overwhelming firepower could not be brought to bear on the landward side of the crater or the interior walls. Here the combination of hand grenades, satchel charges, and bangalore torpedoes reduced the underground complexes one by one. Many were just sealed shut, with their hundreds of defenders entombed forever, like the ancient Hawaiian warriors of the distant past.

The Japanese defenders higher up could see the methodical and deadly process at work on their friends and comrades. Rather than wait for the inevitable and ignoble death that awaited them in the caves, they passed around their last bottles of *sake* and worked themselves into a drunken frenzy. They burst forth from the caves and tunnels in a futile "*banzai* charge" down the slopes into the machine guns and automatic rifle fire, and fell like *sakura*, or cherry blossoms, in the dust. Near four p.m., on December 22, 1945, the American flag was raised on the twelve-hundred-foot-high summit of Koko Crater, marking the fall of the last Japanese command post on Oʻahu. A naval photographer snapped the picture of the flag-raising, and it became one of the most celebrated pictures of the war.

For the prisoners in Diamond Head Crater, the first several days of the invasion had been harrowing. They too had seen the air war for Oʻahu, cheering the downing of a Zero and knowing that air superiority was the first step for ground assault on the island itself. What that would mean for them, they did not know. Over the years of their imprisonment, many of the long-term Japanese guards had grown to have a grudging respect for the stoic endurance of the American prisoners. Some even had a reserved friendship or joking manner with the prisoners, and one or two had formed close bonds, learning English and talking about favorite American movie stars. All of this stopped, however, when word circulated about the presumed American destruction of the Hawai'i Defense Fleet at Midway with a new super-weapon. In their frustration, and realizing the increasing futility of their situation, they began to abuse the increasingly arrogant prisoners as it became clear that America had won the air war as well.

With the landings in 'Ewa and nearby Waikīkī Beach, the guards began to cluster near the machine gun posts. Of course water was cut off as well as food, as both sides eyed each other, watching the balance of power between them begin to change. Anger on one side matched desperation on the other. The anxious prisoners, fearing they would be mowed down like sheep, made reckless plans to storm the barbed wire perimeter, and the guards, sensing something was up, trained their machine guns on the men. Anything could have happened at that point. One false move could have set off a bloodbath of the prisoners just hours before their rescue. Then one of the men, a chaplain, began to sing "God Bless America" in a deep tenor voice, and he was joined by twenty-five thousand more voices. The sound of their singing could be heard over the small-arms fire in Waikīkī. This unexpected and peaceful response completely unnerved the guards, and they fled in trucks and over the rim of the crater, to unknown but certain fates.

The hundreds of prisoners in the Oven were not so lucky. Retreating Japanese troops tossed hand grenades or poured gasoline down into the holds upon the heads of the terrified screaming men, who knew instantly what it meant. The inferno that followed consumed all but a tiny handful of prisoners who were unfortunate enough to be in the ship's holds that week. The smell of charred flesh permeated the air over Pearl Harbor that day.

When American troops arrived to "liberate" the camp, they

were horrified by what they found. Walking skeletons, wearing rags, burned black from the sun, greeted them with cheers, tears, and hugs. A third of the prisoners were down with dysentery, scurvy, and beriberi. All suffered from tropical ulcers, hernias, and gum disease. Many of the American troops had served in the European campaign. They had liberated camps with the names of Dachau, Buchenwald, and Auschwitz, seen the horrors inflicted on the Jews of Europe by the Nazis. Now they had seen similar horrors inflicted on fellow Americans—their friends and buddies and brothers. Filled with rage, they went out and committed outrages of their own on surrendered and wounded Japanese prisoners. Prisoners of the Americans were bayoneted or executed by pistol shots to the head, gold teeth extracted from the dead and dying. The ancient Hawaiian value of *aloha* was hard to find on this day, or on any of the next 885 days of American advance across the Pacific toward the Japanese home islands.

O'ahu had been retaken, at a fearful cost—83,000 Japanese soldiers had died (only 330 taken prisoner) and nearly 15,000 Americans in the three weeks of the assault. Counting the 10,000 Americans killed in the defense of Hawai'i in 1941 and 1942, and the 8,000 who had perished in captivity, 33,000 Americans had given their lives in paradise. This figure did not include the hundreds of civilians who died in the occupation or assault. Hundreds more were to die in the weeks that followed, from wounds, from shock, from hunger and disease. The island was a smoking ruin and charnel house. Hardly a building in the downtown area was left standing. The military bases, American and Japanese, were completely demolished. Not since the great disease pandemics of the mid-nineteenth century had Hawai'i known such misery and horror. Only wartime Manila and Warsaw were more devastated than Honolulu, and that was only because they were larger. Hawai'i had always been a microcosm of change in the Pacific, usually experiencing, first and hardest, the waves of change—disease, missionaries, planters, military, and now war. The Hawaiian god of war, Kū, the god of Kamehameha, was in ascendancy this day. The statue of Kamehameha the Great was untouched and unscarred in the battle that raged around it, while all else, including 'Iolani Palace, lay in smoking ruins.

VOICES

33
Ted's Story: On the Beach 2

April 1947

Dear Flo,

Well, here I am. Two years later I find myself on another beach.

The invasion beaches we hit here in southern Kyushu were mined, and covered with barbed wire just like Kapi'olani Beach was. But this time, I had a rifle. I was with other U.S. soldiers, and they had rifles, too. And heavy machine guns. And we were supported by the gunfire of those ships of the U.S. Pacific Fleet capable of landing shells onshore, as well as flame throwers and amphibious tanks. I still didn't feel more secure.

I felt strange about landing on this beach. This is, after all, the part of Japan that Grandfather came from. Most of the guys in my unit don't know that, and wouldn't care about it if they did. To them, I am Japanese. My potential usefulness as a translator or spy is only occasionally important. More important to them is the thought that I might turn on them at any time. Somehow, they seem to think I might go crazy and kill everyone in some emperor-inspired frenzy. I never try to reassure them. As much as they avoid me, I avoid them. I never play cards with them. Instead, I read books.

But you know by now that I am here for a reason. I wanted to prove to myself, if no one else, that I was American. I wanted revenge on Yoshida. This war is a personal one for me. I just couldn't believe that people from my own ancestral home would treat me the way Yoshida did. I wanted the chance to set them straight, not by working for them, but by showing my loyalty to my chosen homeland—all the way to death, if necessary. I wanted to prove that I would not betray my country. If that meant fighting my "relatives" as well as my enemies, well, I know the story of Minamoto Yoritomo, who had his brother Yoshitsune poisoned for fear he was plotting against him. I know that family betrayal is often best repaid with honor. That is why I joined the American army.

Why they took me I don't know. I was Japanese, and they almost didn't accept my application. But I proved to them that I had been in the Diamond Head prison camp for the entire occupation period. I showed them I had been caught helping the resistance, and they accepted me, and put me on the front line. Now I am part of the biggest amphibious invasion ever attempted, bigger even than D-Day in Europe.

It is huge. It is also eerily reminiscent of the Okinawa invasion. There was almost no resistance on the beach. They practically let us walk ashore.

Oh, there were lines and lines of barbed wire, designed to lead to the easiest points of passage, which were heavily mined with World War I–vintage mines two or three rows deep. This created a few "funnels of death," so to speak, until our sappers could get them out of the ground. People lost their lives here. But there was almost no mortar fire. No big guns, no chattering pillboxes.

The guys who had been in on D-Day in Europe were stunned. They had a constantly hunted look. The more landing craft that came ashore safely, the more afraid they were. They expected all hell to break out, and for us to have to fight our way inland, with bleeding stumps where body parts had been blown off. The near silence scared the shit out of them. They were sure we were being set up.

We weren't. We came ashore with only a few dozen over-turned landing craft and only about 1,000 casualties, with only 134 deaths. It was a cakewalk—right up to the time we reached the first set of hills. Then they let loose on us.

We almost couldn't believe our eyes. No one could shoot. About one hundred boys, somewhere between twelve and fif-teen years old, suddenly jumped up in front of our unit with what looked like bayonets—World War I–era bayonets. They stormed us, screaming *"banzai"* the whole time. They never fired a shot, just came running at us, on tired legs over uneven ground, from about two hundred yards away. By the time they got to us, they were exhausted, and many just fell over.

We realized then that we had no choice, and we started shooting. Not one of them made it to our defensive line. They were slaughtered, the heads and hearts of little boys bursting and shattering like so many ripe watermelons. We were sick to death. Some of the men actually talked about deserting right there. I had never seen such disgust, self-loathing, and fear. I hated myself, and kept seeing the face of a boy I shot, curled into a last, breathless scream, no doubt the only thing he could do to maintain the courage to run headlong into us. His face, still curled in the scream, went down slowly as he clutched the rent in his abdomen my bullets made, trying to hold in the parts that were coming out.

I remembered, at the end of that vision, how empty and hol-low I had felt in my first teenage fight. I was circling my enemy, not ready to fight at all, and wondering how to get out of it, while at the same time not ready to abandon my bravado in front of my friends. That Japanese boy must have felt as I did. Since then, I can't think of him without crying. Tears well up, and I imagine some way I could have avoided shooting. I search my heart, and fantasize about, instead, putting my arms around him, talking with him, teaching him baseball, and surfing.

I remember another incident with a kid. This time, the blood was everywhere. I keep wondering, why didn't they ask me to translate for them? I could have given them the answer they needed, but nobody even thought to ask. I had put down in my paperwork for the army that I spoke fluent Japanese, southern Kyushu dialect. They didn't even ask when they caught this guy, and he was babbling to them, and they couldn't figure out what he said. He was too persistent. I was too silent. I'll tell you about it. Be prepared for some ugly stuff.

A patrol had caught the guy. He'd actually been sneaking around our camp, and it was an embarrassment both to the watch and to the commanding officer that a Japanese soldier had gotten this close. When they brought him in, they asked him if he was alone, and what he had heard. He went into a tail-spin.

He'd been told, he said, by the Japanese government, that the Americans would kill him if they found him, and so if he got left behind or lost, he should commit suicide immediately. Even the lowliest soldier could give away critical information, they said, so a quick death by his own hand was better for the emperor and saved him suffering. It brought honor. But he was only fifteen. He had a girlfriend at home in Okinawa. He wanted to finish high school and learn to be an officer and help design airplanes. He wasn't ready to die. He knew where the Japanese units were we'd been chasing, and he thought he could convince them to surrender—they were all old men and young. They had no more ammunition left. He wanted to take us there.

He kept repeating this, in panicked Japanese, no matter what anyone said. Not one of the haoles in the tent understood him, or brought him a cup of water to show friendliness and just shut him up. The captain had him brought into the tent and searched for papers. Then they asked him if he could speak English. All he said was, "I . . . give out." Then he launched into his plea again.

I was guarding the captain, and was standing outside the entrance to his tent. I kept feeling I should just barge in and translate for them. But the army doesn't do things that way, and I was Japanese to most of the guys in the unit anyway. The only reason they accepted me at all was because they knew I'd been in a Japanese prisoner of war camp in Hawai'i. Most of them thought I'd been a spy there. I often wished I could introduce them to Sergeant Yoshida. So I stayed outside at my post—until I heard the captain say, "Nothing here. Just get rid of him. Take no prisoners. We have to move fast."

So now I've been made point man for the rest of the week. I couldn't keep my mouth shut, Flo. I just couldn't. Now I'm going to have to find more of these kids, while I'm on point, and report them back to the platoon. I don't like this at all. I can see its necessity, but I hate it.

Your brother,
Ted

May 4, 1947

Dear Miss Nakamura,

It is with great regret that I write to tell you that your brother, Private Theodore Roosevelt Nakamura, was killed in action yesterday on the island of Kyushu, in the main Japanese islands. I have enclosed his last letter with this notice. Please be assured that Ted died quickly, and with no pain. You were always in his thoughts, and often on his lips, as he spoke often of his family, and what he wanted to do when he went home. I am sorry to have to bring you this news.

Sincerely,
Lieutenant Jorge S. Serano

VISTAS

34
Operation Olympic

Good day. Today I want to discuss "Operation Olympic," the invasion of Kyushu. The point that interests me most here is that while MacArthur characterized this action as a mission from God, his forces clearly experienced the reality of the Japanese defenses. That reality was that by 1947 Japan was practically unable to defend itself, with five million men stuck overseas in China, or cut off by the American island-hopping campaign. There was really nothing left for defense.

(April 1947)

"Gentlemen, welcome to the most dangerous and the most momentous act of your lives. What you are about to do is nothing less than the accomplishment of the will of God. Your actions, and yes, the sacrifices that you will make—some of you will lose your lives—will help us establish American freedom in the autocratic empire of Japan. Your efforts will bring peace to the earth, in the short term by ending the war, and in the long term by helping us make a belligerent empire into a peaceful democracy. God is with you, and I am behind you. May God bless and keep your souls."

- General Douglas MacArthur, addressing invasion forces

The end of the European war in 1945 had left the United States with significant resources to devote to the campaign in the Pacific against Japan. Documents captured from the Nazis, sorted through and analyzed by American and British intelligence analysts, suggested that Japan may have gained some atomic technology from the Germans.

There was, in fact, some evidence that Japan's infamous Unit 731 had tested an atomic device. High-flying reconnaissance aircraft had picked up residual radiation from a massive release over North China, an area where Unit 731 was known to be operating, and communications from a small city in the vicinity of Yenan had ceased only days before the flight.

Therefore, despite the successful use of an atomic weapon against the Japanese fleet at Midway, the use of atomic weapons in 1947 against the main islands of Japan was deemed too risky. If the Japanese had, in fact, developed atomic weapons, the possibility of retaliation seemed too real. The only option, then, was invasion.

To bring about the unconditional submission of Japan to the forces of the United States, a two-phased invasion plan was devised. The first effort would be directed against the southern half of the island of Kyushu. The United States would secure this island up to a range of mountains that ran across its center, with an invasion force totaling fourteen divisions of army and marines and the full support of the Pacific and parts of the Atlantic Fleet, coming to near two thousand combat vessels plus their support vessels. This large beachhead on Kyushu would be used as the jump-off point for an invasion of the Kanto Plain, the lowland area surrounding Tokyo, the capital of Japan and the residence of the Japanese emperor.

The plan was put into action on July 4, 1946. It started with seven days of naval gunfire to soften up shore positions. The guns were ruthless. Each of the massive sixteen-inch guns on the *Iowa*-class battleships fired a shell equal in weight to a Volkswagen beetle.

The shore of Kyushu erupted from the shelling. The landscape was changed. There was no return fire. As they had on Guadalcanal, Iwo Jima, and Okinawa, the Japanese remained silent—no motion, no communication, no gunfire.

On July 11, the marines and the army went ashore. Hundreds of landing craft and LSTs circled troopships as they loaded, then headed for the beach. Gunners crouched behind their armored shields, waiting for the fight to begin. There was no plunging fire from the shore. Waves caused a few of the landing craft to hydroplane and tip sideways, dumping their crew and passengers into the drink. Most made it out alive and waded to the beach. Only 1,000 didn't make it to the beach, and only 134 never made it anywhere again. They were those crushed by landing craft or victims of clever complementary placement of barbed wire and mines on the beach.

It felt as if Japan had left the front door open. Veterans of the Pacific campaigns remembered Iwo Jima and Okinawa, and groaned inwardly. They knew they would have to wade through blood.

The American forces did encounter heavy opposition in Operation Olympic. Just as had happened on Iwo Jima and Okinawa, and even Oʻahu, the Japanese had holed up in the hills, digging in to the most defensible line they could find and refusing to be dug out again. They did not—by now, really could not—retreat. The Americans had to go at them one-on-one, burning them out of holes with flame-throwers, tossing grenades into caves and under wooden pallets camouflaged to look like the landscape.

Sometimes no one came out. Sometimes, only body parts came out. Sometimes, little children and their mothers and brothers and sisters came out, nearly naked, blinded and stunned by the blast. Many soldiers would never forget the tension, the hair-trigger stress they felt. None of those who witnessed it would ever forget one of the many times when that hair trigger was pulled, and innocent young people died a horrid death.

The Japanese conquest of a quarter of the globe took only four months. In contrast, and in keeping with other late Pacific battles, the conquest of the eastern half of Kyushu took a full three months. Total casualties for the United States were sixty thousand, total dead nine thousand. Appalling, yes, but a bit lower than plans had predicted. The war department had not expected, and so not accounted for, the fact that the Japanese no longer had any serious defenses left. The Japanese defense force on Kyushu consisted mostly of young boys between twelve and fifteen years of age, and men over sixty-five. Neither of these groups had previously qualified for service in the Japanese army. Now they were its main battle force. The reserves and second waves for most of these front-line defenders were far more brutal. They consisted largely of women—of any age as long as they could still run forward—who carried six-foot-long sharpened sticks, with which they attempted to stab at the American soldiers as they ran forward into raging, sorrowful machine-gun fire. When it was done, there was no room to breathe.

Kyushu, everyone knew, including the Japanese High Command, was just a steppingstone. The next and final objective was the Kanto Plain—an invasion that would focus on Tokyo. That one would be the big one.

VIGNETTES

35
The Invasion of Honshu

February 25, 1948. Iwo Jima Airstrip

The twenty B-29's sat in their parking areas, pilots running through their regular checklists, ready to go. Final engine run-ups, the movement of flaps and ailerons in the morning breeze made mechanics keep a wary eye as they ran from tire to tire pulling chocks and saluting the captains of the air crews. A few final promises were made to bring the birds home in one piece—a difficult job in a B-29, even with no war on. Then the radio call came, and the planes began to roll forward in twos. As they reached the form-up altitude, they circled the small volcanic island until the entire flight was in the air, then turned for Tokyo, their bellies full of incendiary bombs.

February 25, 1948.
Asakusa District, Tokyo, Japan

The wind began blowing with its full fury around three in the morning. Those few residents of Asakusa who were just getting up or still awake noticed a clear rise in temperature outside as the howling increased around their rough wooden homes. As

186

they moved to extinguish charcoal braziers on their floors and in their heated *kōtatsu* tables, each and every one of them who noticed the wind marked it as the sign that spring had arrived. The *haruichiban*, the first wind of spring, always brought the season of renewal to Tokyo with a sudden howl of warmth on a cold late winter night. So it was this year. None were aware how much renewal this *haruichiban* carried with it, though. Just as none were aware how sudden that change would be.

But the wind did carry with it the sound, growing every second, of a huge flight of American bombers. The people of Asakusa paid little attention. Theirs was not a factory area. This was all residential, and their growing experience with the American bombers had taught them that military targets were what they were after. So aside from those who began to worry about relatives at work in the few remaining factories in the Tokyo area, most residents of Asakusa stayed in bed. Extra sleep would help them ward off the grinding hunger in their bellies until the calisthenics, designed to do the same thing, and to build strength, and bring out the "Japanese Spirit." The Imperial Rule Assistance Association's announcements said Japanese Spirit could, if properly cultivated, defeat starvation and death. They said it was what made the Japanese a unique people among the nations of the world. It didn't work. But no one said so. They just stayed in bed as long as possible.

They didn't realize the lethal combination that was, at that very moment, plunging toward them to make their lives hell. Incendiary bombs by the thousands would soon ignite homes made of thin, dry wood and paper, the flames fanned by a strong, warm wind. Worse, most of this section of Tokyo had no effective firebreaks. The area around Asakusa and the rest of Tokyo's "Low City" was a tinderbox. Everything went right, as far as the American planners were concerned, and wrong, as far as the residents of Tokyo were concerned, on this night as the horror began.

As the bombs began to crash into homes, shops, and streets,

people forgot their desire to stay in bed, and fled outside, into the maelstrom, down short staircases into holes dug as makeshift bomb shelters as early as 1944. The holes, only about nine to thirteen feet deep, had no other cover besides old wooden doors. They were firetraps. But no one yet knew that the bombs burned instead of exploded. No one yet knew, but they would find out quickly.

The more people streamed out into the street, the more difficult it was to find shelter, until the bomb shelters themselves were so crowded that dozens of people sat directly below the doors, some propping them up with hands, others holding small candles for light.

Then the flames arrived. As the incendiary bombs fell, they burst into lethal balls of burning jellied gasoline. Those that failed to ignite split open on the ground and spread their deadly fuel over several meters. The houses went up immediately, and the fire spread in only a few seconds from every point of impact into an area fully a quarter the size of Tokyo itself.

As the flames grew higher and consumed faster, the panic level of the crowd grew as well. Crowd mentality sent people running like lemmings toward the rivers, the only thing they were sure fire couldn't consume. They jumped in one on top of the other, scrambling for footholds on shoulders to get air. Soon, the river was as full of the dead as it was of the living. As more of the latter were losing the battle for oxygen, the fire reached 1200 degrees Fahrenheit, whipped by the wind into a living frenzy of flame that no longer seemed to burn its fuel. Buildings simply exploded as the super-heated air inside reached dizzying levels of pressure that easily overcame the weakening structures and pressed everything outward. People were reduced in a matter of seconds to charcoal, the water that made up most of their bodies becoming so much humidity in the night air.

The fire, in its frenzy, found a river in its way. Incredibly, it jumped from bank to bank. Not a simple spark carried by the howling spring winds, this was the appearance of fire on one side followed seconds later by its seemingly magical appearance on the other. No flames actually crossed the divide. The heat, the whizzing molecules of air and fuel, simply made the environment on the opposite bank so hot, so fast, that all objects within one hundred feet of the riverbank combusted spontaneously. The sudden appearance of flames on both sides of the river began to cook the bodies still living within it. They were already dead three minutes later, however, since the fire's voracious need for oxygen had caused a vacuum above the water, sucking the last breaths from people's lungs as they so desperately clung to life.

In a parade ground across the river from where the fire had started, twenty thousand survivors gathered, standing on bare ground, not a weed to be seen, in front of a uniform factory. This was the only firebreak they could find in the area, and they hoped it would do.

Their hope was in vain, however, as the same super-heated conditions combined with a sudden gust of the *haruichiban* to create a firestorm—several pillars of fire thirty feet high spinning hungrily about the parade ground, hunting for, and finding fuel. The twenty thousand here all died in three minutes. There was almost nothing left by which to identify the victims the next morning. They simply vanished.

The fire burned itself out after a day, slowly losing its force after the spring wind died down by mid-morning. Hot spots continued burning for a few days, but most of the fire was out by the first evening. Then it was time to find refugees and survivors.

Many of those who did make it through the fire—through miracles, or aided by dedicated relatives who sacrificed their own lives that one or two of the family might live—were totally disoriented and unable to find a way through the rubble to get help. They sat on the side of the road, and many found that digging a small hole in the dirt brought up cool soil with which to soothe badly burned body parts. They discovered too late, in the hospital, that the soil was full of the bacteria that cause tetanus, or lockjaw. Many survivors starved because of a lack of drugs to treat the disease, which causes muscles, especially in the jaw, to seize for days, keeping the mouth so tightly shut that teeth grind and break. The pain of third-degree burns over huge sections of their bodies was only heightened by the fact that starvation was unavoidable.

The allied command, in one extremely well planned and effective raid, had begun to achieve its main goal with this attack. In a state of total war, even the civilian populace was considered the enemy in a strategy developed with Germany and now being refined here in Japan: Kill civilians, in places where they least expect it. Destroy the Japanese ability not just to make the machines and armies that fed the war, but to feed itself, clothe itself, even sleep with any sense of security. By doing this, the Japanese would become not only demoralized, but absolutely incapable of prosecuting the war.

The death of one hundred thousand people in this raid clearly was a surprise for the Japanese and a solid start on that strategy.

April 12, 1948. Kujukuri Beach, Chiba, Japan

Kujukuri Beach stretches fifty miles in a kind of inverted banana shape running from south to north along the eastern coastline of the Chiba Peninsula. All fifty miles were now getting a horrendous pounding.

Four *Iowa*-class battleships, firing sixteen-inch guns that shot massive projectiles, cratered the beach and the coast inland from it for half a mile for seven solid days and nights. They were accompanied by scores of cruisers, destroyers, missile boats and armed marine transports, firing the largest amount of ordnance ever supplied to a naval group in human history. Their goal, of course, was to erase the existence of every living thing along the entire length of the beach.

Kujukuri was the main invasion beach. Yet it was a compromise. One of the main problems the planners faced with this invasion of the Tokyo area on Japan's main island of Honshu was Tokyo Bay. It was a large, shallow inlet that had to be dredged regularly, with only a narrow channel through which major naval vessels might pass without fear of grounding. It was thus impossible to get a full fleet inside the bay to do a preparatory bombardment that might be even minimally effective. In addition, the beaches on the inner rim of the bay were all fishing beaches—generally small, or nonexistent at high tide, many with seawalls to protect the villages from the tsunami waves so common in that earthquake-prone area of the Pacific. Their defenses, while they could be breached, were far more formidable, and made for a far greater likelihood of traffic jams for both men and materiel, than did Kujukuri.

Kujukuri, however, had its own limitations. Along its entire length it was fully exposed to the vagaries of North Pacific weather in a regularly unpredictable season; it was also nearly fifty miles from Tokyo at its nearest point—not a great distance if roads were easily passable. What roads did exist in 1948 between the villages of the Kujukuri area and the capital were rarely paved. All of them wound desperately between rice fields, into and out of other villages, around mountains, shrines, and streams, and finally, after a tortuous journey, into the outskirts of a city that could hardly be described as organized in a grid pattern. All told, on these roads, fifty miles was closer to one hundred. The opportunities for local Japanese who knew the terrain to create effective ambushes, and the difficulty for wide American tanks to follow the paths at all, made this beach only the lesser of two evils in the minds of the planners. At least they thought they could get all the troops and supplies off the ships in a reasonable amount of time. Whether those troops and supplies could get to Tokyo at all was, of course, anybody's guess—which made the quick, and if possible painless establishment of a large and secure beachhead an absolute must for the Americans.

It so happened that, though the Japanese high command knew the Americans were coming (who could miss that, after Olympic), and even guessed the exact location of the main landing, there was nothing they could do to prevent it.

Kujukuri Beach is a long, wide strip of bare white sand, bordered, to the landward, by another wide strip of grass-covered sand. There are very few natural rocky outcrops or mountains that overlook the beach along most of its length. At the extreme north end, near Choshi, and at the south end, near Kazusa, rocky, treacherous harbors provided excellent positions for Japanese forces to weather the firestorm. The main beach, however, provided a clear field of fire for the guns of the great ships. Nothing, it was felt, could survive to fight there. So the Japanese commanders, whose glorification of death in service to the emperor did not extend to stupidly wasting men and weapons, decided to hit them after they got ashore, when the ships couldn't help.

Once again, except for Choshi and Kazusa, the Americans arrived onshore to an eerily peaceful scene. Once again, the quiet took its toll on morale and nerves. Once again, a new line was drawn in the sand with the blood of Japanese and American troops, in a desperate, yard-by-yard slog along the road to Tokyo.

The Japanese defended with what they had. With no gasoline for vehicles, they had to walk or, more commonly, hold their ground no matter what the situation. They fought with World War I–vintage rifles, Lee-Enfields purchased surplus after the French and British exhausted themselves in the trenches between 1914 and 1918. They fought with machine guns garnered from British, French, American, and German sources, also after the Great War. They had almost none of the excellent weapons Japan had produced for its own war in the 1930s and '40s. Those had all been lost or cut off by the island-hopping campaign of the Americans.

The soldiers, like those on Kyushu, consisted mostly of old men and young boys. They were commanded by officers of the home-island defense branch of the Japanese Imperial Army—a branch that had been gutted for the expansion of the 1940s, and one never expected to be put to use in any case. These officers fought with the full realization that this was their only chance to erase the shame of not having served in the empire, or worse, of having been sent back from the front lines—for any reason whatsoever—without serving the emperor with their lives. They commanded boys and men who, however inexperienced and awkward in battle, fought with the sincere belief that they were saving their families. They had been told, and had no reason not to believe, that American soldiers were monsters with huge appetites for causing death. Americans, they believed, would slowly butcher any Japanese soldier caught alive, for no other reason than that they were enemies. Americans loved to rape women, and did so, they were told, especially brutally, relishing the opportunity to cause death, not after the rape to keep the victim quiet, but during the act itself. These monsters were heathens, not a part of the race of the Japanese, who were governed by a benevolent, divine emperor whose ancestors had helped create the world. Americans were not to be trusted, and their rule of Japan would result in genocide. Therefore, if all Japanese had to die, down to the last child, in the defense of the islands, it was no different a result than it would be, they were told, if Japan were to surrender. The only difference would be that fighting to the death would bring honor to the Japanese even as they disappeared from the earth. Surrender would bring a quiet, ignominious disappearance worthy of the cowardice of giving up. The Japanese fought, therefore, not for survival, but for everything—all the marbles. They were small, poorly armed, malnourished, badly trained, and poorly commanded. Yet for all that, they were as tenacious as humanly possible and were willing to take casualties in greater percentages than had even the professional Japanese soldiers the Americans encountered during the island-hopping campaign. Their age or youth made killing them all the more disheartening for the Americans.

So the campaign from Kujukuri to the western outskirts of Tokyo was a slog in every sense of the word. American casualties for the Kujukuri invasion forces alone were near twenty percent. The Japanese lost everyone in every unit that engaged between Kujukuri and Tokyo. Every single one.

April 12, 1948.
Shonan Beach, Kamakura, Shizuoka, Japan

Shonan Beach is a well-protected inlet just outside the western edge of Tokyo Bay. Its naturally dark sand is large-grained, gritty, and soft—very difficult to walk in. It is surrounded by the city of Kamakura, ancient capital of the first shoguns in the twelfth century A.D. It therefore has a long military history.

Shonan Beach had drawbacks that made the Americans decide to land their main force at Kujukuri Beach in Chiba. However, a pincer movement against Tokyo was a large part of the strategic concept for this invasion, and Kamakura was just outside the bay, near a broad enough area of deep ocean to accommodate a bombardment and invasion fleet together. This made it, if not the perfect place, at least a reasonable place for the secondary part of the invasion.

It had its problems, though. Shonan Beach is guarded by a large, rocky island off its center that is a perfect gun outpost. This had to be blasted nearly out of existence by rockets and sixteen-inch shells from the battleship *Iowa* itself. It then had to be watched and taken as quickly as possible so it didn't become a wedge between the invasion forces on opposite ends of the beach, allowing the Japanese to divide and conquer.

Kamakura itself lies in a valley that slopes toward Shonan Beach and is surrounded by steep mountains. This was one of the reasons Minamoto no Yoritomo, the first shogun of Japan, chose it as his capital. A more perfect natural fort almost couldn't be found. It is large enough to be relatively self-sufficient, with its own supply of runoff water in mountain streams, and surrounded by steep hills with limited access and two narrow passes through which forces could travel. All these advantages were secondary reasons the Americans chose to land there. A beachhead established at Kamakura could not be easily dislodged and could be resupplied by sea in the event that the battle for Tokyo became drawn out. But it was essential to take the area quickly.

After the initial bombardment, the Americans went ashore—and again they met silence. It was as if they were filling a power vacuum. The city was completely deserted, the homes of the relatives of the Taisho emperor, father to Hirohito, left empty; storefronts, doors to houses, left open, as if the population of Kamakura had swept out, like seagulls in front of a rising wave. The Americans, uneasy as ever with the lack of shore defense, moved in to occupy and secure the city, but glanced over their shoulders with wary eyes.

Americans, who often put so little store in history, would have done well to know Japan's history that day. Japanese see themselves as their history. They are defined by it, even more so since the encounter with the West that began in 1854 with American Admiral Matthew Perry's Black Ships forcing open Japanese ports. There would have been no surprise if Americans had realized how much Japanese value, and study, their own history.

The Americans were surprised. They didn't know the history of the area. They didn't know that the descendants of Japan's first shogun had been surprised by an enemy army here, an enemy who had descended upon Kamakura from the impossibly steep slopes of the mountains surrounding the town.

The Japanese home-defense-force commander had taken his hint from history. He followed almost exactly what he remembered of the strategy of that brilliant general who had ordered the thirteenth-century surprise attack. This commander had his army, and the residents of Kamakura, abandon their town and move to the mountains as soon as the American fleet began shooting. His strategy was to draw the Americans in, fully expose them, then come at them not from the passes—the doors to the fort—but from the mountainsides, the very walls themselves.

It was a decisive defeat. Battle-hardened, experienced American marines and infantry were driven back into the sea. The loss of life on both sides was tremendous. The Japanese, with their lack of experience and new weapons, fared worse than the Americans. But the win gave a huge boost to Japanese troops all over the Tokyo area. All fought harder because of this victory.

Only the commanders of the Kamakura area, on both sides, knew it couldn't last. The commander of the Japanese forces, against the orders of the high command in Tokyo, abandoned Kamakura again two nights after retaking it. He knew the same trick would not work again, and he decided to preserve what remained of his force for later fights—the urban warfare he knew was coming in the shattered skeleton of the capital city. He moved back toward Kawasaki and Yokohama and set up a series of ambushes that would, in three days time, claim all his men. He himself died with a grenade in his hand, attempting unsuccessfully to negotiate his way under an American tank to make his final act count for something. He was shot before he came close by a 50-caliber Jeep-mounted machine gun. The grenade went off in a rice field, exploding harmlessly behind him.

April 12, 1948. Kisarazu, Chiba, Japan

It was on the fields surrounding Kisarazu, Sodegaura, and Anegasaki, on the inner, bay side of the Chiba Peninsula, that the Japanese army's tank units practiced. Their pitched mock- and live-fire battles had kept residents awake late into the night sometimes before the Great Pacific War had hit high gear in late 1941. Now the fields sat silent. Waves barely covered the mud flats that in low tide provided the only real nourishment the Japanese in this area had left—clams. Thousands of clams and crayfish could be dug out of the muck, and people could be seen for miles up the shoreline walking, stooping, and using three-pronged rakes to try and beat the clams at their own digging game.

It was the job of the LSTs to conquer these mud flats—and any tanks or other armor that lay behind them in the plain around the three villages. They plowed ashore in the early day-light hours, even in advance of the forces on Kujukuri and Shonan beaches. The objective, obviously, was to cut out of any fighting the armored divisions that might be training here at the moment. As had always been the case, intelligence from the main islands of Japan was sketchy, and nothing at all was known about who was present at the training grounds.

As the American tanks and the following infantry patrols with bazookas moved forward in the predawn, they were keen-ly aware of the risk they were taking. There were no battleships offshore to save them if they got into trouble. There were no transports left to take them off the beach. They were on their own, with minimal support, their wits, and the ammo they could carry.

They breathed a collective sigh of relief, therefore, when, after destroying six Japanese tanks parked in a row, they found the fuel tank farm and discovered there was no gas to move the vehicles they saw. From that point on, it was a turkey shoot. There was almost no opposition in the training ground. What little return fire was taken could usually be silenced with a quick bazooka shot to a barracks or other building.

The American assault group thus decided to follow its sec-ondary objective, which was to meet the Kujukuri landing force around the area of Kinshicho, outside Tokyo, to support the fighting there.

April 20, 1948. Imperial Army Headquarters, Roppongi District, Tokyo

Roppongi, or "six trees," is as close to the center of Tokyo as it is possible to get without trespassing on imperial palace ground. In an intellectual sense, however, the most prominent residents of Roppongi had already made that trespass, and the emperor rather liked their presence. The headquarters of the Japanese Imperial Army was here. Today, army leaders were trying to find a way to address the most pressing issue they had ever dealt with.

They were being pressed, that day, from two sides. Americans who had retaken Kamakura had pushed through Yokohama and Kawasaki and were now on the outskirts of Tokyo, in an area known as Shinagawa, the former embarkation point on the Tokaido Road to Kyoto. In the east, the Americans had passed Kinshicho, crossed the Edo River, and were now marching across the barren landscape of what had been the "Low City"—the Asakusa area and its surroundings.

The home-defense force had been continuously annihilated during attempts to stop the barbarians and keep them from getting near the emperor. It seemed the only choice now was to call on the citizens. The problem was, there were not many left in Tokyo—perhaps two hundred thousand. They would be required to bring whatever weapons they could—the Imperial High Command had nothing to give them now—and sacrifice their lives in an attempt to drive the Americans from the shores of Japan.

Some in the planning room actually believed that a *kamikaze*, a divine wind like that which had saved Japan from the Mongol hordes in the thirteenth century, would arrive again, and flatten the American devils into dust. Others went along because it was the line they had taken throughout the war, and they could find no way out of it now. In any case, there was no disagreement in the room, and the call went out to residents of

Tokyo. A second call went out to the outlying areas to tell people to prepare to resist the Americans everywhere.

April 21, 1948. Showa Avenue, Tokyo

The American forces halted as they came up to Showa Avenue. They stopped because they saw something the likes of which they had never seen before: nearly twenty thousand Japanese, armed with clubs made of short table legs, spears made from broom handles, even brooms themselves. They stood and looked at the Americans, just as the Americans looked at them.

American commanders, all on the horn with each other immediately up and down the line of advance, were busy discussing what to do. Neither side attacked. The Americans had no desire to continue killing unarmed Japanese, and these were not even soldiers, but young children, women of all ages, the disabled, armed only with crude weapons. This was almost as far as you could stretch the call of duty, most of the commanders felt. If asked, their troops would kill these people, then mutiny in protest. American soldiers could be brutal, but there was a place where that brutality stopped, and that was likely right here, at the potential mass murder of effectively defenseless civilians. They were at an impasse, and they were unsure how to continue the advance.

The Japanese commanders behind the lines of civilians in Tokyo, pleased at the effect their new soldiers had on the enemy, took this as a sign of American weakness and began urging the people of the capital to attack, to throw themselves at the Americans.

The civilians didn't move.

The Japanese commanders became more shrill. "Serve the emperor's wishes," they screamed. "Die well, and you will die with honor, for yourself and for Japan!"

The civilians stayed put. But they were talking. Suddenly, in a slow, painful ground swell, they began to mill about. The Americans put rifles to shoulders.

The mob began to move backward. It was gruesome to watch as some of the slower—to move or understand—were trampled. But the focus of the crowd's attention was clearly changing. They had turned around, and now they were rioting. They began to pull the Japanese officers who commanded them down onto the street and beat them to death. They began to burn buildings, especially police stations, and pull down the imperial insignia wherever they found it. When the military police, and the thought police, arrived on the scene, they, too, were surrounded by the crowd, and the wave of crowd violence began to move toward the Imperial Palace.

April 29, 1948.
A concrete bunker,
Imperial Palace Grounds, Tokyo

A stylus slowly ground grooves into the rotating wax disk on the turntable beneath it. The Showa emperor, ruler over the era of "Great Peace," spoke slowly into the microphone in his nasal voice, addressing the Japanese people directly for the first time ever. In his formal, nearly incomprehensible Japanese, he told the nation that the militarists had finally been defeated. That the Japanese military and the courageous stand of subjects against the American army had freed him, the emperor, to make the decisions necessary to bring peace to Japan.

He asked his subjects to "endure the unendurable" and accept a military loss to the United States. He personally would hold accountable every surviving member of the army and navy General Staffs for the needless deaths of millions of loyal Japanese subjects in this useless war of aggression. He begged the Japanese to accept the occupation of the Americans with equanimity, and with the positive knowledge that sometime in the near future the Japanese would again control Japan and help him guide them toward their true destiny.

The war, he said, was over.

VIGNETTES

36
Ka'ahumanu

May 1948. Windward O'ahu

"Your granddad, he give you dat name cuz you seem so stubborn when you wuz born. Wouldn't hardly come out. So he call you by the name of the most stubborn woman he could think of: Ka'ahumanu."

The words echoed in Ka'ahumanu "Connie" Fortuno's mind. Few knew the significance of her name beyond the Hawaiians here—and there were so few of them left. But she knew. It trapped her, in a sense. No one had expected less than she herself that the name would lead her to the spot she stood in now. But her name was her destiny. She'd started this, hardly thinking what she was doing. She'd just acted on the memories of her grandfather, Kaleo Kekaula—*kahuna*, wise man, and advisor to the king—when he could act no more. He'd been too old to endure the arrest and mishandling by American troops rounding up "collaborators" after they reconquered the islands. He'd been too weak of heart to bear the destruction his beloved O'ahu had been subjected to as the Americans and the Japanese slugged it out for final control of the Hawaiian chain. He'd been too disappointed that the restoration of the Hawaiian king,

Stephen Kamāmalu, under the Japanese occupation had no time to work itself out into full independence and nationhood for Hawaiʻi.

Her grandfather had been a realist, but one with a dream. He knew from the start that the restoration of the monarchy by the Japanese commander, Mori, had been a ruse to gain the cooperation of the local Hawaiian population. But, like Emperor Pu Yi of Manchukuo, he had been a firm believer that in time, the ruse could be made reality. The Japanese, he reasoned, could be worked with. They hadn't, after all, annexed Hawaiʻi immediately after its surrender in February 1942—even though they could have. Instead they had given the islands, in nominal fashion, their independence, provided they worked with the Japanese Empire. He had seen that there was some sincerity in the Japanese slogan "Asia for the Asians," and that they included Hawaiʻi in their concept of Asia. They had even redistributed the land. They'd taken away what had belonged to the Big Five—those millions of acres—and provided everyone who wanted one a plot of land big enough to grow enough food to survive on, and even a bit of a surplus. The land had bloomed.

When the Americans came to the house to take her grandfather away, he said to her quietly and quickly, before they came inside, "Remember our promise at the top of Haleakalā. The kingdom of Hawaiʻi must see the sun again."

In her sudden surprise and fear of the Americans, she had given little thought to his words until later that night, when she heard the radio news. The so-called king of Hawaiʻi, the American announcer said, was under house arrest. The United States government would, as part of its postwar reform program, try the king as a collaborator with the Japanese enemy. Further, the Americans refused to end martial law by May, though there was no serious disobedience or sabotage, as there had been under Japan. They were going to return any "illegally redistributed land" to its "rightful owners." The process of sorting out who owned what land before the invasion, and who would stay where they were, was to begin by mid-July. The inheritors of the Big Five were in town and were wasting no time organizing dinners and meetings with the staff of the occupation government, making certain their claims were already being heard informally. She had even seen them with blueprints, standing on the roadsides, surveying, planning, getting ready to retake the economy. Their manner was brusque toward most Hawaiians.

These events had moved her to action. The ancestors had called her name down through time. She had to act to save her grandfather's dream, his king (now, she decided for certain, he was her king, as well), and her people from one more conquering army. There had been enough death and destruction and mutilation of the land. The people of Kamehameha had seen enough violence done to their population, their culture, and even their language. She decided she would see Hawaiian independence in her lifetime—real independence that did not rely on a beneficent conqueror. But the way had been unclear. War was out of the question. There were not enough Hawaiians to make an army, and she wasn't sure whether others—Japanese, Chinese, Filipinos—would join them. Besides, they had no weapons, and so had no way of standing up to the conquerors with violence. She wanted no part in sponsoring a mass suicide to make a point that was meaningless if no one survived to be independent.

The only way open was peaceful agitation. She had read of an Indian lawyer named Gandhi who had begun to organize Indians against their British colonial masters. He talked about a type of civil disobedience, *ahimsa,* in which the Indians, in groups, actively broke the laws that restricted their freedoms, but did not do so violently, and neither resisted, nor assisted, the authorities who came to arrest them.

This kind of protest might work. If she could enlist the support of most of the people who had been living in the islands since before the war, and get them to disobey the Americans until they gave up and went home, then Hawai'i would belong to itself. She would talk with Japanese, Filipino, and Chinese leaders as well as those who led her own people. She was sure they would see the logic of her idea. They had to. They all could lose if they didn't work together.

She realized that civil disobedience could easily get out of hand. Especially in a state of martial law, where the Americans could easily apply violence, and where trials were really only a formality, this would require strict rules of behavior. So she began to set them up in her mind.

No protester would be allowed to use violence, either against people, buildings, land, or objects. There had been enough destruction. She would base this rule on the idea of *aloha*. Love people, even when you disobey them, she thought. Treasure the land—the *'āina*—for it is our greatest gift. Do not destroy the things people have lovingly built up. Honor them, and they will honor you. However, since this was to be disobedience, it was almost a certainty that the Americans would arrest, and even beat, demonstrators. Those people were to refuse to go, but not to resist violently. They could do whatever it took to stay in place, short of striking out against the arresting person. If they were dragged away, so be it—they should not stand up and walk away. They should refuse to provide names and addresses of themselves or any others. But they should not defend themselves against violence or take part in violent action of any sort. Stand firm. That had to be the motto.

June 1948. Pearl Harbor

As Connie (she used that name, she said, for the benefit of non-Hawaiians who found her real name hard to pronounce; privately, she admitted to herself, the full weight of the name Ka'ahumanu was a heavy burden that she didn't want to deal with every minute during a tense situation) looked over the human chain, she felt satisfied. A line of people, two deep, blocked each gate into Pearl Harbor. The total number to start was around twenty thousand demonstrators, and they joined hands at each gate to prevent the crossing of any vehicle. They were determined to keep the Americans inside their human cordon. They chanted *oli*, sang folksongs, and waited as the sun rose over the old tank farm, slowly moving across 'Aiea, burning down on the airfield at Ford Island, before moving into full force on the 'Ewa side of the shallow harbor. They carried long *maile lei*, beautiful in their green leafiness, traditionally not tied together at the ends. They were held lengthwise, along the line, and one began where the last ended, making this cordon, in a very real sense, a human *lei*. Connie liked the feel and the sound of that. This was a movement to free Hawai'i, symbolized by traditional Hawaiian signs of *aloha*. Inherent in the *lei* was a feeling that there was to be no violence here.

At about ten in the morning, the military police came out to test the situation. They probed the line at three different gates, getting a feel for how organized the protesters were. In each case, two MPs in a Jeep asked those blocking the gate to move. When no movement occurred, the MPs threatened arrest. Upon realizing that the protesters were not fazed by the threat, this test crew was, in all three cases, gone within five minutes.

At eleven o'clock, a large group of Japanese brought their own *maile lei*. These long-time islanders, many the next-door neighbors and friends of the Hawaiians in the line, were given space and a place. As the morning wore on, Filipinos, Chinese, more Japanese, and even some haoles, both residents and mainlanders who supported the islanders' goals, showed up. Nearly all (except the haoles) were descendants of sugar plantation workers. Nearly all had received some land in the "Second Great Mahele." None wanted to see things change now that they had what their ancestors had so long hoped for them. Their political organizations, invited by Connie, had made the decision to support this peaceful movement for freedom.

By noon, the waiting game was getting difficult. Placards

and sign-holders near the gates held messages that made the protesters' goal clear. "Freedom now," one read. Others read "End Colonialism, Practice Liberty" and "Practice what the Declaration of Independence Preaches."

Connie came along the line, encouraging people, speaking here and there to keep spirits up. She was dressed in a traditional *mu'umu'u*. Over her shoulders was draped a *lei* of beautiful local flowers, and the crown of her head was encircled with a halo of sea grape. When she moved along the line, she walked—though she could have taken a car. Her progress was slow. But it gave her time to show *aloha* to nearly everyone in the line. She was generous with her gratitude.

By one o'clock the violence began. The army sent a troop-transport to each gate. Their mission, the troops were told, was to clear the gate and maintain an open route from each gate onto Kamehameha Highway. Do what it takes to get the job done. Don't kill anybody.

The trucks unloaded within twenty yards of each gate, and platoon commanders moved their men up in an orderly fashion. As the protesters were commanded to move aside, more transports pulled up at each gate, and MPs jumped out in large numbers, truncheons and handcuffs at the ready. When the protesters refused to go, the action began in earnest. MPs ordered people to "spread 'em" for body searches. Demonstrators refused. MPs and soldiers then manhandled them up against trees, threw them against the fence, used truncheons to slap knees out from under them. Once down, protesters refused to answer questions or present their wrists for cuffing. They refused to get up, once their arms had been wrestled into the cuffs, and refused to walk to the waiting transports. They had to be dragged, usually by two or more of the military personnel.

The frustration level grew within the army—from the grunts on the ground right up to the unit commanders, who had to continually order more men to the scene—since it took two MPs to arrest and manhandle one protester to the waiting trucks, and the line filled in any gaps almost immediately.

By one-thirty, violence flared. The frustration level had reached a breaking point on both sides. When Connie, who had moved two-thirds of the way around the perimeter of the crowd, began chanting an *oli* to keep spirits up, several MPs, at all three gates, broke. The swiping of legs became more concentrated and more purposeful. The swipes were fast, to make the falls harder. Any who resisted too often became potential targets for batons to the head, shoulders, kneecaps, and even faces. Blood began to flow from mouths and legs. But still the protesters held.

A tall and powerful Hawaiian man, his neck weighed down in *lei* so thick you couldn't see the flesh, had to be dragged by five servicemen. They had to shoulder and holster their weapons in order to use both hands and the full strength of their bodies. The dragging of this man to the truck alone took nearly twenty minutes, and the MPs were exhausted when they went back toward the protesters. They wanted to rest, and with the urgency that such a feeling brings, the cracks of their truncheons against knees and shoulders grew that much sharper and that much more powerful as they waded back into the mass.

But every time a protester was take away, a new person stepped in to take the empty space. No matter how many of the *maile lei* were ripped from hands, they never seemed to disappear, or even to fall all the way to the ground.

June 1948, 1:53 p.m. Pearl Harbor

One MP, a veteran of the war, who'd seen friends on Okinawa and Iwo Jima die—to pay for the freedom of these protesters, he thought—found himself alone in the midst of a group of them. No one made a violent move at him, but neither did they open a way for his escape. "Save the king," they shouted. "Freedom for Hawai'i!"

What did they think they had? The islands had been liberated, brought back into the United States. What more did they want? They got protection, they got American-style freedom—true freedom, from the MP's perspective. So he was frustrated beyond reason when a protester stuck his face in close and shouted, "We were better off under the Japs than we are now!" That was it. This lousy guy was going to get a taste of what it cost for him to be a part of the USA. Americans had lost their lives for this guy. He could feel himself reaching for his weapon.

The silence was utter. The world was still. The crowd had no idea how to react, and the MP found himself standing over the body of a dead man. Blood and brains littered the sidewalk and those in the spatter path. In a moment that seemed like eternity, the MP realized what he had done. As he did, his gun spun slowly on its trigger guard around his limp finger and found its way to the ground, clattering and breaking the silence. The crowd began to back away. Two of the protesters with spatter on their faces and clothes began to blubber incoherently. The MP just stood there—tears staining his cheeks. He had no excuse. That was all he could think. No excuse. As his colleagues slowly slipped handcuffs around his wrists, gently talked to him and led him away, all he knew was that two lives had been wasted.

Finally, as he sat down in the passenger seat of a Jeep, he realized that Hawai'i was not free. That the losses his friends, his brothers in combat, had accepted to make these islands and Asia free, meant nothing if the people could not choose for themselves who they wanted to be. And they could not choose, he knew now, without more violence. The thought saddened him beyond all description. Then his thoughts turned to his family.

Ken Jones, a photographer for *Life* magazine, stood in bewildered silence. He'd photographed Okinawa. He'd been on the beaches of Operation Olympic, the invasion of mainland Japan. He'd seen indescribable horrors, photographed them, and lived to tell about it. He was a believer, too, in the sacrifice that American servicemen had made to free this land, and all the lands of Asia and the Pacific. He never believed he'd see this. He was sick with rage and sorrow. Sick with the physical remains of the event. Sick with timidity. He knew he had the photo. He knew he had to leave now, or be asked for the film. He knew, outraged or not, that the last thing he wanted to do was stay and face the MPs and the crowd. The last thing he wanted was to see more violence.

He'd come here on assignment as a lark. A few days in Hawai'i, where the sun always shines, and the death and destruction were limited, covered over by a veneer of recon-struction, since Hawai'i was the main forward base for U.S. Pacific operations. He'd come for the beach and the tropical drinks. Now this. He ran. He wanted a bar, he wanted a bath, and then he wanted a fast, safe, courier plane out of here for his film. Then, he thought, journalist's ambitions never far from the surface, he wanted to find out who organized this thing— and why they didn't fight back.

Ken's photos, published in *Life* and sold everywhere on the mainland, whipped up a frenzy of public anger and a large amount of sympathy for the idea of Hawaiian independence.

August, 1948. Fort Shafter

The crowd was huge. Large enough to sit, cross-legged, with *maile lei* strung together, in front of the main entrance to the base some five people deep. It consisted of people of Hawaiian, Japanese, Chinese, Filipino, and European ancestry. They held signs that said "Free Our King," and "Stop the Show Trial." One placard even said, "A summary execution would be more honest," in red letters. They sang songs, chanted, and clapped their hands. They were in good spirits. They were fac-ing outward.

Connie Fortuno stood at the head of the crowd, at the main entrance to Fort Shafter. It was fully blocked, as were all the other entrances, with people, and with homemade barricades. She stood, defiant, smiling, waiting.

As the motorcade carrying Stephen Kamāmalu, recently restored king of the Hawaiian Islands, now once again common citizen of a territory of the United States and newly accused collaborator with the Japanese occupiers, drove into sight, it slowed slightly. Military police stopped, exited their cars, and stood facing Connie at the gate.

An admiral, in navy dress whites, stepped out of one of the limousines and walked directly up to Connie. Neither he nor she was fazed as the MP commander yelled, "Officer on deck," and the MPs snapped to full attention.

"At ease," the admiral said. "Miss Fortuno."

" 'Connie' is sufficient, Admiral." She replied.

"Connie." The name did not roll off his tongue easily in this situation. "I have a prisoner who is scheduled for trial here this morning. He is accused of treason against the United States of America during wartime. I require you, under the law of the said United States of America, of which Hawai'i is a territory, and currently under martial law, to allow this motorcade to enter and begin the process of bringing the prisoner to justice."

"Admiral, we will not allow you to pass. You may attempt to force us to leave, but we will not go willingly."

"Connie, this is a violation of the law, and may also be an act of conspiracy against the United States. I ask you again, having fully warned you of possible arrest and trial for you and every person here, to move aside and allow this motorcade to enter."

"I tell you again, Admiral, that we will not allow you to hold the trial of King Kamāmalu. Arrest us if you must. Be aware that there will be many to replace us. We will not allow this to happen in our islands."

To the MPs the admiral said, "Gentlemen, carry out your orders." He strode back to his limousine.

The MPs immediately handcuffed Connie. At that moment,

211

she began to chant. The entire crowd joined in. She began to collapse toward the ground. One of the MPs had hold of her wrists, and her sudden collapse took him by surprise. As he countered her fall with his own strength, and with the only grip on her he had, her shoulder dislocated and she howled in pain. Then she went back to the *oli*, her face ashen, taking her cue from those around her, who had continued to chant. They had to drag her, rather than lead her, to one of their cars. She was practically thrown into the back seat.

Ken Jones got it all on film.

The admiral watched out his car windows. He was certain that without this Fortuno woman to lead them, the crowd would begin to disperse. He waited two hours. No one left. The protesters were sometimes silent, sometimes chanting. They were constantly defiant, even after their leader had been driven away to jail—and to anonymity, he hoped. They stayed.

He sent four MPs to clear the drive. They arrested ten people in short order, all of whom had to be dragged away in handcuffs, some requiring a whipping across the shoulders with a billy club to get them to show their hands for cuffing. The rest filled in the gaps, and the motorcade was unable to move through.

It was noon when the admiral finally gave up. The trial time had passed two hours before. He gave the order to take the prisoner back to his cell, and the motorcade passed by Fort Shafter. As it did, a huge cheer rose up, grating on the admiral's nerves. He thought of driving around the block, and looked out his rear window as they drove off. No one left their places in the crowd. No riots, no masses breaking to go home and fix dinner. Today was a loss. Chalk it down, he thought, and be patient. The winner would be the one who could wait longest.

Ken Jones got it all on film.

January 21, 1954.
Partially restored palace of the kings

One dozen soldiers lined the walk to the main entry of the newly rebuilt palace of the kings and queens of old Hawai'i. One dozen soldiers in khaki, rifles on shoulders, uniforms as crisp as the morning breeze, stared straight forward, standing at parade rest in eerie silence as the Stars and Stripes was lowered from the flagpole. The only sound, heard by those closest to the flag crew, was the clinking of hooks against each other, and a shraaap shraaap that sounded like the closing of drapes on a silent Sunday afternoon. Thousands of onlookers, from every part of the Hawaiian Islands, looked on from streets, buildings, and the parade ground in front of the palace. All were silent. All were straining to see and hear.

When the flag was down, it was folded in the traditional triangle. Silently, the officer in command of the color guard, Lieutenant Kamai, of the King's Guard, turned sharply on his heels, took two steps, and placed the flag in the hands of the lieutenant governor of the Territory of Hawai'i. He then turned again, sharply.

Facing the one dozen, he called, "Attention!" He turned toward a man in a flowered shirt and nodded. A small group of Hawaiian men in traditional dress began to chant as a new flag was raised on the pole outside the palace. This was the flag of the kingdom of Hawai'i, flown last in 1893, risen, again, like a phoenix from the ashes of two empires.

The one dozen stood unmoving. Their hands went up in crisp salutes. A tall, dark-haired man in a dark formal suit, standing at attention on the balcony, appeared to be crying. As the *oli* ended, he stepped to the rail. "The time of troubles is over," he said, clearly audible in the silence and the morning air. "As a result of the courageous defiance displayed by the people of Hawai'i, protesting without violence in the true spirit of *aloha*, placing a boycott on all goods from the United States, and refusing to allow them to try me for treason against a nation whose authority over these islands we do not recognize, I hereby proclaim that Hawai'i has chosen its course. The kingdom of Hawai'i is restored!"

The 'Iolani Palace was engulfed in a deep silence. Trade winds whistled past the still onlookers, ruffling hair, turning tired eyes to the view of Honolulu Harbor. There, in the distance, Aloha Tower stood, rebuilt, the clock in working order, a new monument standing at its base telling the story of Hawai'i's independence. Beyond it was the sea. No naval vessels were moored in Honolulu Harbor. The bay was nearly empty, but for local fishing boats. They were all, every one, moored securely. The fishermen, for this event, had come home.

"My first act, as king of these islands," said Stephen Kamāmalu—looking, from up close, somewhat the worse for wear after several years in prison, well treated as he had been— "is to honor the person who made this possible. Only one person had the *aloha* and the persistence, the love for us all, to bring us together in pursuit of our purpose. I honor as a national hero our second Ka'ahumanu. Ka'ahumanu Fortuno. Please accept our gratitude."

With that, he hung a stunning *lei* around the neck of Connie Fortuno, who couldn't hold back her own tears as the shouts of triumph went up from the crowd. Her grandfather's dream. His Hawai'i. Her part, she thought, had been small. His part had been to inspire it all. As she stood, speechless, she could think of nothing else to do but smile at the king, her eyes averted, and step back.

Ken Jones got it all on film.

VISTAS

37
The Last *Samurai* in Paradise

I would like to begin my final lecture in this series with a news story published some twenty years after the war.

"It has been reported from Honolulu, Hawai'i, that a Japanese soldier today walked out of the Ko'olau Mountains above the city of Honolulu on the island of O'ahu—twenty years after the end of World War II. Details are sketchy at this time, but it appears the report is credible, as other stubborn fighters have surfaced on Guam and the Philippines in recent years. Camera crews from around the world, especially from Japan, are on their way to Hawai'i, and a special representative from Emperor Hirohito will also make the journey to greet this long-forgotten war hero."

Associated Press, August 6, 1968

Atsushi Noda began the last day of his single-handed struggle with America in the usual way—a ritual bath in the small pool of his favorite fern-shrouded stream. This was followed by a brief ritual in the little Shinto shrine he had carved into the soft lava rock, so well hidden all these years. Very few devotees of Shinto, the animistic nature worship of ancient Japan, had ever lived as close to nature, in nature, as Noda. Indeed, he had almost become a *kami*, or spirit, himself. The beauty of the Ko'olau forests and streams and cliffs had long ago burned away any hatred of the Americans, or the desire to harm anyone.

He was here because he was ordered to be here, and as a good soldier of the emperor, he followed his orders. Noda had been trained in intelligence gathering. Unlike the infantry, taught to blindly follow orders, up to and including a suicide *banzai* charge, Noda was required to think independently in situations where there were no fixed rules. He was intelligent, stoic, and strong-willed, and his determination and principles as a recruit led to his selection for this special assignment. He had been called in to Imperial Headquarters in Honolulu on the day the American invasion armada had been spotted.

His orders were simple—stay alive and hidden in the mountains, gathering information on the American enemy in case their assault against O'ahu was successful. Under no circumstances was he to take his own life. His responsibility was to collect intelligence on the enemy until such time as Japanese forces could return for him, even if it took three to five years. His commander explained that this would require conduct normally considered disgraceful, but he said to himself, "These are my orders; I shall carry them out. If it is to the slightest use to my country, I shall be happy. I will fight on in my own way until that day of my country's return." Noda just had time to pack his survival gear and be dropped off near the top of Tantalus, overlooking the city, when the American assault began.

With his powerful binoculars, he was able to see the vast armada of ships gathered off the 'Ewa plains. The belch of flame and smoke from the battleships' big guns was followed by a thunderous roar and explosion on the shore. "This beautiful landscape," he thought sadly, "is going to become a battle-field."

He was familiar with both the beauty of Hawai'i and the horror of war. He had been in the first assault wave landing on the North Shore, slightly wounded in the shoulder, but surviving grim firefights where most of his comrades perished. He became convinced that he was purposely spared for some great assignment like this one. He became entranced with the natural wonders of the islands, and he spent his spare time hiking in the mountains and along the shores of O'ahu. While his fellow soldiers caroused in the bars of Waikīkī or the bordellos of Chinatown, Noda explored O'ahu, and when he had the chance, hopped a plane or ship to the outer islands, disappearing into the valleys, craters, and lava fields for days at a time. He often met Hawaiian fishermen or hunters who took a liking to this affable young man who could even speak some Hawaiian. They showed him edible plants and sealife, how to make snares and fish traps. No Japanese national knew the Hawaiian Islands as intimately as Noda, and this is why he was picked for this special assignment. He disappeared into the forest as the LSTs streamed ashore off the 'Ewa plains.

Going deep into the rain forests of the Ko'olau Mountains, Noda missed the horrible carnage in the final battle for O'ahu, but occasionally, climbing a tree or high clearing, he could see the beautiful city disappearing under a swirling cloud of smoke and dust, like a funeral shroud, in the incessant rain of shot and shell. When, after a few days, the gentle trade winds blew away the pall of black smoke, he was saddened to find virtually nothing left of the city but piles of blackened rubble. During the night, the breezes off the ocean carried the stench of death and decay far up the slopes overlooking the city. Noda had seen enough destruction close up to know what had happened, and he withdrew deeper into the mountain forests and began his lonely, last assignment.

In the ensuing years, he was occasionally sighted by pig

hunters, hikers, or those gathering rare Hawaiian plants for hula or medicinal purposes. Usually, however, he spotted others first and quietly withdrew to one of his many hidden caves or fern glens, and even the hollows of giant banyan trees. He had developed a circuit of campsites across the leeward face of the Ko'olaus, always with an escape route up the mountainside through a dry streambed or rocky crevice. His principal "residences" were two—one in an ancient Hawaiian burial cave and the other in a tree house—at either end of his circuit. The burial cave, which he had stumbled on after a year in the mountains, was an old lava tube. It was filled with ancient bones, carved wooden idols, feather cloaks, and an assortment of stone tools. In its dry recesses, he stored his gear and made his sleeping area. The tree house was entirely his own creation. As a boy, he had been fascinated with Japanese translations of *The Swiss Family Robinson* and *Robinson Crusoe*, and when he came across the giant banyan, he knew immediately what he had to make, even at the risk of discovery. Except for the sheets of tin he managed to steal from a half-completed chicken coop, the hidden tree house was made entirely from nature, from plans created in his own inventive mind. He spent many contented days in this well-hidden spot overlooking eastern O'ahu.

Noda lived primarily on mangoes, bananas, papayas, and coconuts, with protein in the form of wild birds, stream fish, prawns, and an occasional chicken lifted from Filipino farmers in the back of Kalihi Valley. He called the necessary forays "stepping out for the night." He also, regrettably, "liberated" clotheslines and rubber raingear, a small radio, batteries, soap, and matches. He was nearly caught several times when the dogs barked, and was shot at on more than one occasion. Stories spread of a "wild man" in the mountains. The Filipinos called him a "mountain devil," and for the Hawaiians he was a *menehune*, one of the ancient little ones of old Hawai'i.

So Noda passed the years, refusing to believe the war was over. He was outside the stream of time, sure only of the world of 1945. He had been taught that the Japanese Greater East Asia Co-Prosperity Sphere would take "a hundred years of warfare" to establish, and the years he was giving were only a tiny part of the sacrifice of the Japanese people. The occasional magazine he came across with pictures of Japan convinced him the war was still going on, and going well for Japan. From the pictures of rising skyscrapers and freeways full of cars, he could see that Japan was clearly thriving and prosperous. And of course, if the war was lost, then everyone in Japan would be dead—*ichioku gyokusai*, "100 million souls dying for honor"; that slogan was on everyone's lips when he last went home on leave. If one person were left alive, Japan could not have surrendered, he thought.

Closer to his mountain and forest home, Noda watched the slow rebuilding of Honolulu, but it was nothing like it had been before the war. Two-story wooden buildings replaced the concrete and steel structures of the business district, making the whole city resemble the Chinatown of old Honolulu. Very few new cars appeared; the old ones—1930s and '40s models, were just repaired and restored. Just as he was, the makes and models of the cars were stuck in time. Curiously, the new ones were mostly from Japan, and their license plates read "Kingdom of Hawai'i."

From his limited knowledge and memory of the past, Atsushi Noda constructed an imaginary world that fitted with the oath he had taken. For all the years he was alone, it was a static world of fixed ideas. The real world came upon him late one afternoon in the form of a daring Japanese honeymoon couple who came to the pool to skinny dip. They found him dozing naked in his favorite fern-glen pond. He was not a young man anymore. The years of hard living had taken their toll. Often now he had to rest to catch his breath, and he found himself dozing off unexpectedly. Before he realized what had happened, they had snapped his picture, and called out to him in Japanese before he made his escape. Suddenly his resolve faded, and he turned to face his astonished discoverers holding only a fern leaf across his middle. There were no snakes in Hawai'i, no serpents now in the Garden of Eden. It was as if Adam and Eve had come across Rip Van Winkle! He followed them meekly down the trail to their rental car and sat in the back seat as they drove down Makiki Heights and back into the stream of history.

The delighted couple drove him to the office of the Japanese consul, where he solemnly handed over his sword when they assured him, yes, the war was really over. He gritted his teeth at the waste of twenty years of his life, but compared with the ultimate sacrifice of many of his comrades, it seemed insignificant. Suddenly his mind was flooded with thoughts of home and family—thoughts he had deliberately put aside twenty years ago. The consul made some hurried calls to the restored 'Iolani Palace and to the press. Noda was given a clean, newly pressed Japanese military uniform, circa 1944, and a chance to shave and shower in a bathroom for the first time in two decades. For the first time also, he slept in a real bed. In the morning, the royal government of the kingdom of Hawai'i rolled out the red carpet for this man from another time. The new young king, still just a baby when Noda went into the mountains, greeted him warmly. The Hawaiian Royal Guards saluted him smartly as he strode down the front steps of the palace and into the backseat of the old open-air limo for a grand tour of Honolulu and O'ahu, now the capital of an independent island kingdom.

The city was, as he had seen from a distance, shabby and slightly dilapidated. Although there were a few cars in the street, most people used the new trolley system that ran through the city. Low-rise, two-story wooden buildings had taken the place of the Big Five headquarters buildings and banks on Bishop and Merchant Streets. They and other multinational corporations and businesses were nowhere to be seen in Hawai'i. Noda noticed there were very few Caucasians in the streets now. The languages he heard on the sidewalks were mainly Hawaiian, Japanese, and pidgin. The survivors of the war had gone home, and postwar politics in the islands guaranteed they would likely not return in any numbers, except for Marxist university professors and their radical, sandal-clad students. They were here to see the "great new dawn of socialism." The Hawaiian kingdom had been nicknamed the "Cuba of the Pacific," since its legislature was dominated by the left-wing labor unions. They had taken over island politics in the wake of the American withdrawal after independence a decade earlier. The People's Labor Party (PLP) had begun some of the social-engineering schemes for which the Left is so well known, and the political pilgrims from Europe and the United States wanted to be a part of it. They saw of course only what they wanted to see. Although the Hawaiian government retained the American Bill of Rights in its new constitution, there had already been erosion around the edges, with political prisoners in the old Sand Island internment camp. One consequence of the loss of both the Philippines and Hawai'i as forward bases was that the United States had not become involved in the civil war between communist and noncommunist forces in French Indo-China. (Noda of course could understand none of the Cold War terminology or references—"Cuba of the Pacific," "containment," "mutual assured destruction." He was completely baffled when told that Japan and Germany were firm allies of the United States against their former allies—China and Russia.) Noda was saddened to learn that his home island of Hokkaido had been occupied by the Russians since the closing days of the war.

Despite the machinations of the American Central Intelligence Agency, the PLP, led by the dockworkers union, had followed a policy of nationalization of big businesses, driving out foreign capital in the process; "poor but proud" was the unofficial motto of the PLP. The big political issue at this time was the debate over whether to lease Pearl Harbor to the Soviet

Union in exchange for much-needed financial assistance. Despite the lure of money, the prevailing sentiment in Hawai'i was to remain part of the nonaligned nations in the Cold War between the United States and the Soviet Union. It was never to be forgotten that the presence of military bases and the American Fleet in Hawai'i had led to the terrible destruction in the Great Pacific War.

The PLP had maintained and even extended the land reform process started by the Japanese military government during the occupation. Noda could see this as he toured the countryside; small farms dotted the land, replacing the waving fields of sugarcane and stands of pine. Now rice, taro, bananas, and sweet potatoes covered the land. The islands appeared to be on their way to self-sufficiency once more. Hawai'i in 1968 looked more like the Hawai'i of 1768 than the Hawai'i of 1938. If Kamehameha the Great had come back now, he would have felt right at home. (Another feature the king would have recognized was that the new PLP aristocracy had replaced the feudal *ali'i* of the great king's time, with power and privilege accruing to the "new class" of party bureaucrats and functionaries as it had all over the socialist world.)

As the motorcade came around to the North Shore and down the windward and south coasts of O'ahu, Noda could see more and more evidence of the war. Scores of abandoned bunkers and pillboxes dotted the shore—too massive and too expensive to tear down, sitting now covered with vines and sand dunes. At the turnoff to the Hawai'i Defense Highway through Hā'ikū and North Hālawa valleys, he saw a plaque in memory of the hundreds of POWs who died in the construction of the railway and tunnel. He thought he could see artillery shell holes on the cliffside below the Pali Lookout, where he helped on the assault there. Passing Makapu'u Beach, the party entered the East O'ahu Battlefield Park. There, a shrine on the high cliff memorialized those hundreds who threw themselves off rather than surrender and risk captivity at the hands of

American forces. Large expanses of this area were off limits due to unexploded ordnance. On the surrounding coral reefs, divers still found the wreckage of planes and landing craft. As for other sites, money for a cleanup was not to be found. The seaward face of Koko Crater was pockmarked with shell holes from American battleships, and bones were constantly turning up everywhere. Hawaiians stayed away from this place at night, for they said the new Night Marchers were out then—the countless ghosts of the nameless struggles in these hills. Now, on the twentieth anniversary of the end of the war, both Japanese and American visitors—former veterans on both sides, and their families—were returning to Hawai'i to see the sites of their former struggles, assignments, or captivity. Japanese visitors scoured the cliffs, caves, and gullies for the bones of their brave soldiers. The remains were cremated in traditional Buddhist ceremonies. A fledgling tourist industry was starting, based on family–owned-and-operated bed-and-breakfasts. The big hotel chains had not been able to get a foothold since the PLP had come to power, and Waikīkī was rebuilt as a quaint collection of cottages and bungalows.

As the king's motorcade approached Diamond Head, Noda asked His Majesty for an opportunity to stop at three specific sites. The first was the Diamond Head American National Cemetery, maintained by the American government. Inside the crater, thousands of white crosses marked the final resting places of the POW dead, and countless more from other Pacific Island battles. The next stop was the Japanese Imperial Cemetery and Shrine, inside the Punchbowl Crater. The giant black slab of stone marked the burial site of the ashes of thousands of Japanese war dead from the final battle for O'ahu. How many beautiful memories and awful nightmares disintegrated here with these bones and ashes? How many millions of unlived years lie buried in these numberless graves, and in the thousands of other war cemeteries around the world? How many doctors and scientists, poets and lover that will never be?

How many shattered survivors and unborn children, never to experience the beauty of Hawai'i? The tragic waste and violent absurdity suddenly overwhelmed him like a great wave.

The last stop was the Royal Mausoleum—the resting place of all of Hawai'i's monarchs save two. Here, the newest tomb was that of Steven Kamāmalu, who died young, as most Hawaiian monarchs did, shortly after the Hawaiian struggle for independence was achieved. Beside him was a small plaque above the urn containing the ashes of General Mori, honored by burial here for his policies of restoring both the monarchy and the land to the people of Hawai'i. After a few minutes of silence alone, and a prayer, Atsushi Noda turned to leave. He was suddenly very weary. For him, the Great Pacific War was finally over. It was time to go home.

As the old soldier shuffled out of the royal cemetery, a butterfly landed on the white marble slab of the king's tomb and fluttered its wings. A few molecules of air lifted off into the Hawaiian sky.

Afterword

I apologize for the more personal, less Olympian final lecture in my series on the making of the modern, independent kingdom of Hawai'i. The reason for this, as many of you know, is that the late Atsushi Noda was my father. I wanted to view the postwar changes in Hawai'i through his eyes, as he was a part of the story.

My father was twenty-three years old when he landed here with the Japanese invasion force in 1942. He was forty-six when he came out of the Ko'olaus and finally surrendered—the last *samurai* in paradise.

He was an instant celebrity back in Japan—for fifteen minutes, as they say. The older generation looked at him with a mixture of honor and guilt; they knew what it had all meant. The younger generation looked at him with curiosity and incomprehension. They could not guess how someone could be so dedicated to such a mission.

His fame quickly faded as the media searched for new fads, fancies, and personalities. Even though he was considerably older than the ideal age for marriage, my father had lots of offers. He married my mother, and they started our family, late in life, but not significantly later than many other Japanese had in the immediate postwar period. Because of our age difference, my father was more like a grandfather to me when I was a child. But he told me stories every night about his adventures in Hawai'i during the Great Pacific War.

These stories sparked my own interest in the war, and in Hawai'i, and when I decided to become a historian, I naturally specialized in modern Hawai'i. My father lived long enough to see me receive my Ph.D. from Sophia University in Tokyo. By the time of his death, the nation he had served so long and so honorably had largely forgotten him, as it had chosen to forget most other veterans of the war and even as much of the war itself as possible. Therefore, the invitation by the Royal University of Hawai'i to present this lecture series was a gift from heaven. This has been a great opportunity, on this sixtieth anniversary of the attack on Pearl Harbor, to remind the world of the effect the war had in Asia and the Pacific.

I have used the microcosm of the Hawai'i experience, both under the Japanese occupation and during the American counterinvasion, as a metaphor for the tremendous social and political changes that the war set in motion throughout the Asian and Pacific regions of the globe. First among these, perhaps, and well illustrated by the Hawai'i experience, was the collapse of the European colonial system and the rise of indigenous, often radical independence movements. This was hardly what the Japanese planners had in mind when they launched the moves that would culminate in the formation of a Greater East Asia Co-Prosperity Sphere. History rarely works according to the whims of its human planners.

Recent theoretical models, including interpretations of so-called chaos theory, suggest that tiny changes at critical moments can alter the space-time continuum, thus, obviously, impacting history. This only brings home, in my mind, the fact that the way the world is at this moment is not a given. Only a few events occurring in a different order, or with slightly different results, would likely mean that the present would be radically different.

Consider this: What if *Enterprise* had not been in Pearl Harbor on the morning of December 7, 1941? There was a storm brewing that day; if it had occurred just a couple of hours earlier, it might have delayed *Enterprise*'s arrival until well after the Japanese air raid. Admiral Halsey might not have been killed during the attack. Fears of the American carriers launching a surprise attack might have caused Admiral Nagumo to cancel the third wave of bombings, thus leaving the fuel storage depot intact and the channel in and out of Pearl open. The Japanese in such circumstances might not have felt an invasion of Hawai'i was feasible, and there is every possibility that Hawai'i would now be still a part of the United States of America.

History can play strange tricks. The possibility I've just described indicates to me that we should be careful how we look at cause-and-effect relationships, in the past, and in the present. There is no inevitability.

Explanatory Notes

Most of the major actions, events, and policies described in this book are based on actual occurrences throughout Asia and the Pacific during the Great Pacific War:

• The restoration of the monarchy and the land reform program are based on Japanese occupation plans for Hawai'i (see Stephan, *Hawai'i Under the Rising Sun*).

- The third wave attack on Pearl Harbor was strongly urged by flight commander Fuchida, and later by Admiral Yamamoto.

- The descriptions of Hawai'i's defenses are taken from the facts and statistics of 1941.

- The Japanese invasion of O'ahu is similar to those of Luzon and Malaya.

- The defense of the Mōkapu Peninsula parallels that of Bataan.

- The *banzai* and suicide charges happened at Guadalcanal and Saipan.

- The prisoner march and atrocities in Waikīkī are based on the Bataan Death March and the Rape of Nanking.

- The American fallback to the West Coast is part of the U.S. War Plan Rainbow Five.
- Japanese defense fortifications for the North Shore are based on fortifications at Tarawa, the Marshalls, Palau, and New Guinea.
- The Hirohito Line and Koko Crater defenses are like those of the Shuri Line on Okinawa and Iwo Jima.
- The prisoner of war camp in Diamond Head had real-life counterparts at Camp O'Donnell and Cabanatuan in the Philippines, Woosung in China, and Changi in Singapore.
- The prison ship descriptions reflect the shipment of POWs to Japan under terrible conditions; sometimes the ships were sunk by American plane and submarine crews unaware that American prisoners were aboard.
- The introduction of State Shinto and new Japanese immigration were Japanese policies for the Micronesian Mandated Islands.
- The Hā'ikū tunnel project corresponds to the Burma-Siam railroad.
- Coast watchers were important in the Solomon Islands campaign.
- The description of the nuclear air burst over the fleet at Midway is drawn from descriptions of the Bikini Atoll nuclear tests.
- The destruction of Honolulu in the American invasion mirrors the fate of Manila.
- The mass suicides occurred on Saipan.
- The land invasion of Japan is based on General MacArthur's Operations Olympic and Coronet.
- The Hawai'i independence movement draws inspiration from Gandhi's nonviolent struggle in India.
- The "last *samurai*" in the Ko'olaus is modeled after the

Japanese holdouts on Guam and the Philippines who emerged twenty and thirty years after the war.

- And the whole direction of the Pacific war between America and Japan was foretold by Hector Bywater in his 1925 book, *The Great Pacific War* (see Honan, *Visions of Infamy*).

To paraphrase the professor character in the movie *Back to the Future*, "Great Scott, we've altered the Space-Time Continuum!" In order to set the historical record straight, we offer the following chapter-by-chapter notes, which should make clear what in this book is real and what is fiction:

Chapter 1

Meteorologist Edward Lorenz is credited with discovering the "butterfly effect," or "the sensitive dependence on initial conditions," a central concept of chaos theory.

The carrier *Enterprise* was not at Pearl Harbor at the time of the Japanese attack on the morning of December 7, 1941. She was two hundred miles away, having been delayed by a storm on her return from a trip to reinforce Wake Island. *Enterprise* was in fact due in to Pearl Harbor at six on the morning of December 7. We have simply assumed that the storm did not occur.

The carrier *Lexington* was also not present in Pearl Harbor that morning. Returning from a reinforcement run to Midway, it avoided discovery by the Japanese fleet, though it was probably closer to the attackers than any other vessel in the U.S. Navy. Since it avoided discovery, it was never damaged by attacking planes.

There was no third wave of attack from the Japanese air fleet. Although it was planned, Admiral Nagumo decided against launching it, fearing the arrival of the missing American carriers *Enterprise* and *Lexington* and the potential presence of American submarines.

Admiral William (Bull) Halsey, in command of *Enterprise*, was not killed on December 7. He, together with Admiral Nimitz, was the architect of the American advance through the central Pacific and the use of aircraft carriers as the primary fleet weapon of the U. S. Navy. Halsey, commander of the Third Fleet, and Admiral Chester Nimitz advanced through Micronesia simultaneously with General Douglas MacArthur, who escaped from the Philippines to Australia, and who led the American offensive through the southwest Pacific—New Guinea back to the Philippines ("I shall return"). American forces converged on Okinawa in 1945, and the battle there was the bloodiest of the Pacific war. Halsey died peacefully at home in 1959.

The fuel depot that now exists beneath Red Hill on Oʻahu was built after the Japanese attack on Pearl Harbor. The Japanese targeted, and missed, a large fuel depot located roughly between Hickam Field and the east shore of the harbor. The United States quickly realized after the attack that such an open-air fuel depot was vulnerable, and moved it. The fuel storage in that tank farm contained all the marine bunker (fuel) that the U.S. Pacific Fleet in Hawaiʻi had, and made Hawaiʻi the only U.S. Navy refueling base between California and the Philippines. Had it been destroyed, as we suggest, the United States would have been strategically crippled in the Pacific Theater.

Chapter 2

The Hawaiian monarchy, overthrown in 1893, has never been restored. This act was, however, in the Japanese plans for occupying Hawaiʻi. There was no Stephen Kamāmalu, but there were and still are claimants for the crown.

Chapter 4

Hawaiʻi was not isolated by the Japanese subs, but rapidly became a fortified, invulnerable forward American base for attacks against Japan. In the six months after the Pearl Harbor attack came the Battle of the Coral Sea, the Doolittle Raid, and the Battle of Midway. After Midway, the first major land offensive was the epic Battle for Guadalcanal. It is likely that Hawai'i could have been seized by Japan immediately following the crippling of the American Fleet on December 7, 1941.

Chapter 6

"Eastern Operation," the Japanese invasion of Hawai'i, was actually planned by the Japanese to follow the anticipated destruction of the rest of the American Fleet at the Battle of Midway. Instead, it was the Japanese Fleet that suffered irreversible losses at Midway on June 4, 5, and 6. Japan lost four carriers, all of which were involved in the Pearl Harbor attack, and hundreds of skilled pilots. The American carrier *Yorktown* was also lost at Midway, the turning-point battle of the Pacific war.

Chapter 8

Admiral Chester Nimitz did not perish in an escape attempt from Hawai'i. He replaced Admiral Husband Kimmel after Pearl Harbor and with Admiral Halsey led American naval forces to ultimate victory in the Pacific war. Nimitz died in 1966.

General Delos Emmons, who replaced General Walter Short after Pearl Harbor, did not die at his command post. He remained in command in Hawai'i during the martial law years, which continued throughout most of the war and long after the Japanese threat to Hawai'i had disappeared. Martial law in Hawai'i was declared unconstitutional by the U.S. Supreme Court and finally lifted in July 1944.

Chapters 10 and 12

The Diamond Head Prisoner of War Camp did not exist, but it is based on descriptions of POW camps throughout Asia and the Pacific. (See Daws, *Prisoners of the Japanese*.)

There was an internment camp at Sand Island for several hundred AJA prisoners.

Chapter 14

There was no Rev. William Kamaka or Camp Roosevelt, but Kanaka is based, of course, on Father Damien of Molokaʻi and his ministry at Kalaupapa.

Chapter 16

There was no Second Great Mahele giving the land back to Hawaiians and Japanese, but there was an original Great Mahele in the nineteenth century, which had the effect of alienating the Hawaiian people from the lands. The statistics used in this chapter are accurate.

Chapter 17

Togo and his family are fictional characters, but it is known that Admiral Yamamoto was familiar with the writings of Hector Bywater, especially *The Great Pacific War*. Yamamoto and Bywater met each other in London in 1934 at a naval conference, and it is clear that Bywater's ideas had a profound influence on Yamamoto.

Chapter 18

The descriptions of the Japanese defenses on Oʻahu, as noted, were based on descriptions of other Japanese island fortresses: Tarawa, Kwajalein, Peleliu, Iwo Jima, New Guinea, and Okinawa, all taken by American forces at great human cost.

The Hāʻikū-Hālawa tunnel was not built by POWs under the Japanese. Its described location is that of the controversial H-3 highway constructed in the 1980s and '90s.

Chapter 20

Coast watchers and saboteurs were active throughout Japanese-occupied islands such as the Philippines and the

Solomons. The lives of many, including the young John F. Kennedy, were saved by the coast watchers and their islander allies.

Chapters 26 and 28

General Mori is a composite of several honorable Japanese commanders, and Lt. Kimura is based on a brutal Lt. Colonel Tsuji, responsible for atrocities throughout the Pacific.

Chapter 29

Midway Atoll was seen as strategic by both the United States and Japan and, as noted, was the site of a decisive, turning-point battle in June 1942. It was a carrier-based naval and air battle, not a nuclear one. The American atomic bombs were used against Japan in the destruction of Hiroshima and Nagasaki in August 1945.

Enola Gay, the aircraft that carried the bomb that razed Hiroshima, was a B-29, apparently one of the most difficult planes of the era for a pilot to handle.

Chapter 32

In our battle scenario, we list 15,000 Americans dead. To put this into perspective, nearly 20,000 Americans were killed in the invasions of Iwo Jima and Okinawa. Over 100,000 American soldiers, marines, and sailors were killed in the Pacific Theater—slightly more than one-third of total American deaths in World War II.

More than 150,000 Japanese and Okinawans died in the assault on Okinawa alone, and more than 1.5 million Japanese soldiers were killed in the Great Pacific War. Almost 50 million people died in World War II, more than four times the number of World War I!

Chapters 34 and 35

Operations Olympic and Coronet were the planned land

invasions of Japan, scheduled for late 1945 and 1946. The atomic bombing of Hiroshima and Nagasaki, together with the Russian declaration of war against Japan, forced the Japanese surrender on August 15, 1945, saving millions of lives.

Tokyo and other Japanese cities were heavily firebombed, killing more people than died when the atomic bombs were dropped on Hiroshima and Nagasaki.

Chapter 36

There was no second Ka'ahumanu who led the Hawaiian independence movement, but there was a first—the favorite wife of Kamehameha the Great. She overturned the *kapu* system and is known as one of the most influential women in Hawai'i's history.

In 1954, Hawai'i did not become independent, but in that year the Democrats finally captured control of the Territorial Legislature (and have been in control ever since). Nineteen fifty-four is thus seen as a "revolutionary" year in Hawaiian history.

Chapter 37

Atsushi Noda, who hid out in the Ko'olaus for twenty years, is a fictional character based on Hiroo Onoda, who hid for thirty years on the island of Lubang in the Philippines.

The Russians seized northern Sakhalin Island, not Hokkaido, from Japan.

There was no People's Labor Party, but the Left-led ILWU did make a bid for power in Hawai'i following World War II in the 1949 dock strike and in an unsuccessful attempt to take over the Democratic Party. Hawai'i is not quite the "Cuba of the Pacific," but does enjoy a reputation as an antibusiness, big-government state.

Punchbowl is of course the American Cemetery of the Pacific, with its honored dead of the Great Pacific War and later wars. And perhaps by the flutter of a butterfly's wing, Diamond

Head remains the geographic symbol of a tourist paradise, and not a POW hell.

SOURCES AND RESOURCES

Bailey, Beth, and David Farber. *The First Strange Place: Race and Sex in World War II Hawaii.* Baltimore: The Johns Hopkins University Press, 1992.

Brown, DeSoto. *Hawaii Goes to War: Life in Hawaii from Pearl Harbor to Peace.* Honolulu: Editions Limited, 1989.

Daws, Gavan. *Holy Man: Father Damien of Molokai.* Honolulu: University of Hawai'i Press, 1973.

_____. *Prisoners of the Japanese: POWs of World War II in the Pacific.* New York: W. Morrow, 1994.

Dorrance, William. *O'ahu's Hidden History: Tours Into the Past.* Honolulu: Mutual Publishing, 1998.

Dower, John. *War Without Mercy: Race and Power in the Pacific War.* New York: Pantheon Books, 1986.

Fuchs, Lawrence. *Hawaii Pono: An Ethnic and Political History.* Honolulu: The Bess Press, [1992] 1961.

Goldstein, Donald M., Katherine V. Dillon, and J. Michael Wenger. *The Way It Was: Pearl Harbor, the Original Photographs.* Washington, DC: Brassey's, 1991.

Honan, William. *Visions of Infamy: The Untold Story of How Journalist Hector Bywater Devised the Plans That Led to Pearl Harbor.* New York: St. Martins Press, 1991.

Hoyt, Edwin. *Japan's War: The Great Pacific Conflict, 1853–1952.* New York: McGraw Hill, 1986.

Kimmett, Larry, and Margaret Regis. *The Attack on Pearl Harbor: An Illustrated History.* Seattle: Navigator, 1992.

Marcellow, Ronald E., and Robert S. La Forte, eds. *Remembering Pearl Harbor: Eyewitness Accounts by U.S. Military Men and Women.* Wilmington, DE: SR Books, 1991.

Ogawa, Dennis. *Jan Ken Po: The World of Hawaii's Japanese Americans.* Honolulu: University of Hawai'i Press, 1973.

Onoda, Hiroo. *No Surrender: My Thirty Year War.* Translated by Charles S. Terry. New York: Kodansha International, 1974.

Peattie, Mark. *Nanyo: The Rise and Fall of the Japanese in Micronesia.* Honolulu: University of Hawai'i Press, 1988.

Pfannes, Charles, and Victor Salamone. *The Great Battles of World War II.* Vol. 1, *The Pacific Island Battles.* New York: Zebra Books, 1985.

Prange, Gordon William, Donald M. Goldstein, and Katherine V. Dillon. *God's Samurai: Lead Pilot at Pearl Harbor.* Washington: Brassey's, 1991.

Salomon, Henry. *Victory at Sea* (television series and book). New York: NBC News, 1952–1954.

Skate, John Ray. *The Invasion of Japan: Alternative to the Bomb.* Columbia, S.C.: University of South Carolina Press, 1994.

Smurthwaite, David. *The Pacific War Atlas, 1941–1945.* New York: Mirabel Books, 1995.

Spector, Ronald. *Eagle Against the Sun: The American War with Japan.* New York: Vintage Books, 1985.

Stephan, John. *Hawaii Under the Rising Sun: Japan's Plans for Conquest After Pearl Harbor.* Honolulu: University of Hawai'i Press, 1984.

Stillwell, Paul. *Air Raid, Pearl Harbor! Recollections of a Day of Infamy.* Annapolis, MD: Naval Institute Press, 1981.

Takaki, Ronald T. *Pau Hana: Plantation Life and Labor in Hawai'i, 1835–1920.* Honolulu: University of Hawai'i Press, 1986.

Toland, John. *Infamy: Pearl Harbor and Its Aftermath.* Garden City, NY: Doubleday, 1982.

About the Authors

Richard Ziegler earned a B.A. in History at Allegheny College and an M.A. in American Studies at the University of Hawai'i at Mānoa. He was a Peace Corps volunteer on the island of Ponape in Micronesia from 1968 to 1970 and has traveled widely through Europe, Asia, and the Pacific. Since 1975, he has been a professor at Honolulu Community College, where he received the Regents' Medal for Excellence in Teaching for 1999–2000.

Patrick M. Patterson holds B.S. and M.A. degrees in History (with a specialty in Modern Japan) from the University of Oregon. A resident of Japan for five years, he currently teaches history at Honolulu Community College.